Reading detectives

Year 6

one; A m... walking,
...on on the ground, ...ring on a
...home t... his wife and gave her
... it?' ...id not a thing. It's
..., As it glowed on h... f...
...t midnight they woke.
...a chill voice cried. 'Wha... ...illa...
...on't worry, m... ...ear. ...aw...
...eleton opened t... door. ...
...floor. 'What was ...at, William. ...
...my de... ...'ll soon ...away.' ...
...imbing th... ...' The ...illed...
...er her head. A ... ...a chur...
...The waves had... ...t gra...
...g, l... ...a ske...
...a ...e ran h...
...ou get it?'

Author and Series Editor: Rachel Clarke

How to use this book

This book has been written to address the rigour of the National Curriculum and KS2 Statutory Assessment Tests for reading. It contains:
- 15 high-quality extracts from a range of genres, which can be used in any order
- in-depth questions that encourage pupils to look beyond literal interpretations of texts and to delve for more complex meaning by using contextual clues and literary devices
- two pages of detailed teaching assessment for each text.

A Close Reading Chart is provided as a prompt to support pupils when undertaking reading comprehension. This can be copied for display in the classroom or included in pupils' work books.

The breadth of questions

The book aims to replicate the style of questions found in the KS2 Reading SATs. Questions from across the reading content domains are included, but with a particular focus on inference and deduction, which is often challenging for pupils.

KS2 Content Domain reference	
2a	give / explain the meaning of words in context
2b	retrieve and record information / identify key details from fiction and non-fiction
2c	summarise main ideas from more than one paragraph
2d	make inferences from the text / explain and justify inferences with evidence from the text
2e	predict what might happen from details stated and implied
2f	identify / explain how information / narrative content is related and contributes to meaning as a whole
2g	identify / explain how meaning is enhanced through choice of words and phrases
2h	make comparisons within the text

At least three questions for each extract are taken from Content Domains 2a–2c, with at least one focusing on vocabulary. The remaining questions focus on Content Domains 2d–2h.

The book recognises the importance of vocabulary for reading comprehension. It focuses on:
- knowing the meaning of words
- making inferences based on words used
- being able to identify and evaluate how the choices of vocabulary enhance meaning.

To help pupils gain a greater familiarity with the language used in SAT questions, the book uses phrases such as 'locate' when asking pupils to 'find the place' and 'which word suggests…' or 'what impression…' when asking them to infer meaning.

Teaching and assessing

As well as providing answers to the questions, the teaching assessment notes refer to the Content Domain being assessed. Whilst there is no Working at Greater Depth descriptor for reading at KS2, the book recognises that some pupils will respond with greater degrees of analysis. For this reason, many of the questions covering Content Domains 2d–2h are accompanied by extension answers.

About the texts

The selected texts are demanding but not beyond the pupils' abilities. They enable pupils to:
- experience vocabulary outside their usual experience
- encounter descriptions and imagery produced through deliberate word choices
- tackle grammatical structures that are challenging and unfamiliar.

Contents

Romulus and Remus: Twin Boys who Founded Rome
by Geraldine McCaughrean — Traditional tale — **Page 5**

When Hitler Stole Pink Rabbit
by Judith Kerr — Historical fiction — **Page 10**

The Purple Lady
by Jamila Gavin — Fairy tale — **Page 15**

I am Malala
by Malala Yousafzai with Patricia McCormick — Autobiography — **Page 20**

The Visitor
by Ian Serraillier — Poetry — **Page 25**

The Mystery of the Clockwork Sparrow
by Katherine Woodfine — Historical fiction — **Page 30**

Arthur: High King of Britain
by Michael Morpurgo — Legend — **Page 35**

The Cloudspotter's Guide
by Gavin Pretor-Pinney — Non-fiction — **Page 40**

Five Children and It
by E. Nesbit — Classic literature — **Page 45**

Oddiputs
by Nicholas Fisk — Science fiction — **Page 50**

Africa: Eye to Eye with the Unknown
by Michael Bright — Non-fiction — **Page 55**

Fenn Halflin and the Fearzero
by Francesca Armour-Chelu — Modern fiction — **Page 60**

Cowboy Song
by Charles Causley — Poetry — **Page 65**

The Great Adventures of Sherlock Holmes:
The Engineer's Thumb
by Sir Arthur Conan Doyle — Classic literature — **Page 70**

The Tempest
by William Shakespeare — Play script — **Page 75**

CLOSE READERS:

 Read the text slowly at least twice

 Get the gist of what the text is about

 Circle words they aren't sure of and try to figure them out

 Reread, annotate, and underline key vocabulary

 Use the text to answer questions

 Gather evidence from the text

 Talk with each other about what they think it means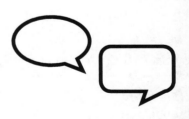

 Read again to summarise or answer specific questions

Romulus and Remus: Twin Boys who Founded Rome

Empires rise and fall. The gods, who can see the future, know these things. That is why the gods of Greece gradually shifted ground to the skies over Italy. They came to be known by different names: not Zeus but Jupiter; not Hera but Juno; not winged Hermes but winged Mercury.

Around the shrine to Vesta a great temple was built, its 'vestal' priestesses the unmarried daughters of good families. Because all their love was promised to the goddess, they were forbidden, on pain of death, to give any love to a man.

Rhea Silvia did not: mortal men she could easily have resisted. But the god Mars – quarrelsome Mars, warrior-wild and handsome as only an immortal can be – wooed Rhea Silvia like war besieging a town. He blasted her with love, bombarded her with tender words, shot her full of passion. She could no more resist him than the flowers on the altar could resist the flames which ate them.

Finding she was pregnant, she tried hard to hide her secret, but soon her slim figure grew as round as a sail, and the other priestesses whispered behind their hands, "What is to be done? Rhea Silvia has broken her vows! Rhea Silvia is giving birth … to twins! Rhea Silvia must die!"

Her mother and father were important citizens – descendants of Aeneas himself. They might have pleaded for the life of their daughter or spirited her away to safety. Instead they upended their hearts and emptied out every last drop of love they had ever felt for her. "Bury her alive, as the law demands," they said. "Rhea Silvia must die."

"But the babies? The twin boys! What will become of them?"

"Throw them into the River Tiber! The pity is that they were ever born!"

Brick by brick, Rhea Silvia was sealed up in her tomb, those last bricks shutting out the sounds and sunlight of the living world. Mars could have shattered her prison with a single breath, but he had long since left Latium to batter some other lady's heart or to raise up war in the world.

As for the twin boys – Romulus and Remus – they were carried naked in a basket to the banks of the Tiber. The servants sent to carry out the task would have tipped them in, midstream. But the Tiber was in flood and the waters milled by with such terrifying force that they set the basket down on the muddy shore and watched till the swollen river swirled the children away towards a watery death.

Ah, but weren't Romulus and Remus the sons of Mars, the descendants of Aeneas? Though their tiny pink fists and feet were powerless to save them, they were strong, healthy boys. The cold did not kill them, nor the river spill them, nor pike snatch them down to a muddy death. The basket was swept helter-skelter downstream until it snagged on tree roots and spun into a backwater where the wild creatures came to drink. A face loomed over the crying boys – a mask with yellow eyes and a mouth full of ravenous teeth. The wolf opened her grinny jaws, seized on first Romulus, then Remus, and ran with them to her lair. There she dropped them among the soft, tumbling fur of her hungry cubs …

And there she suckled them, letting them drink, as her cubs drank, from her soft, warm underbelly. A woodpecker perched on a branch nearby to keep watch for danger. (If this seems strange past belief, you should know that wolf and woodpecker are creatures sacred to Mars.)

A herdsman found them. Out one day hunting the wolves who threatened his livestock, he found two big, squalling baby boys, pink and brawling in a wolf-den, and took them home. Now the herdsman was no fool: he knew full well who they were – knew that the law had demanded their death. But he and his wife had no children of their own, and neither civic duty nor fear of punishment counted for anything alongside the joy those children brought them.

Perhaps Romulus and Remus drank down the ferocious courage of the she-wolf as they drank her milk. Perhaps they learned courage and endurance from her as she came and went, feeding and fighting for her young. Or perhaps, as sons of Mars, there was already warrior blood in their veins. But Romulus and Remus grew up into brave, quarrelsome boys who never shunned a fight and who never lost one either.

No shepherd life for them! No life in peaceful Latium. Even before their father told them the story of their birth, they were roaring boys, with roaring friends, their sights pinned on glory. They set their hearts on building a new city, a grand city, a city to rival Troy or Carthage or Athens.

Romulus and Remus: Twin Boys who Founded Rome by Geraldine McCaughrean

Questions

1 Which of these words is **not** a synonym of *'squalling'*?

crying   howling   agitated   blubbering   wailing [*1 mark*]

2 Decide whether each statement about the extract is true or false.   [*1 mark*]

	True	False
Rhea Silvia's parents were related to Aeneas.		
Mars rescued Rhea Silvia from the tomb.		
Romulus and Remus were raised by a wolf.		

3 What is meant by *'the Gods of Greece gradually shifted ground to the skies over Italy'*?
[*1 mark*]

4 Which repeated word indicates the author's uncertainty about where the twins' characteristics came from?   [*1 mark*]

5 What is implied by *'A woodpecker perched on a branch nearby to keep watch for danger. (If this seems strange past belief, you should know that wolf and woodpecker are creatures sacred to Mars.)'*?   [*1 mark*]

6 Copy the phrase that suggests that the twins' heritage meant that no harm would come to them in the river.   [*1 mark*]

7 Which words and phrases does the author use to reinforce the description that Mars wooed Rhea Silvia *'like war besieging a town'*? Why do you think the author chose to do this when writing about Mars?   [*2 marks*]

8 What impression does the word *'brawling'* give you about Romulus and Remus's relationship with each other?   [*1 mark*]

9 Do you think that Mars was villainous? Give a reason for your answer.   [*1 mark*]

10 The actions of other characters determined what happened to Romulus and Remus. Find **two** examples in the text of how this statement is true.   [*2 marks*]

Teaching assessment

Supporting pupils to read and understand traditional tales

When answering questions about traditional tales, encourage pupils to read the extract all the way through first. Encourage them to think about what is happening in the story, noticing who the main characters are and where the action is taking place. Pupils should look for features commonly found in traditional tales, including seemingly impossible challenges, moral lessons and repetition of phrases. Pupils are now ready to think about how the writer has used language to develop the characters and their relationships with each other. They should underline the important descriptive words and put a circle around any words they are unsure about. They may be able to work out what these mean from the context. Pupils are now ready to start answering questions about the text.

(1) agitated   **1 mark** (Content Domain 2a)

(2)

	True	False
Rhea Silvia's parents were related to Aeneas.	✓	
Mars rescued Rhea Silvia from the tomb.		✓
Romulus and Remus were raised by a wolf.	✓	

1 mark for all three correct (Content Domain 2c)

(3) The Gods moved from Greece to Italy.   **1 mark** (Content Domain 2a)

(4) The author repeats *'perhaps'*, which shows her uncertainty about the source of the twins' characteristics.   **1 mark** (Content Domain 2g)

(5) Expected standard: To answer this question, pupils should be able to infer that the presence of the wolf and the woodpecker implies that Mars was protecting his sons.

1 mark (Content Domain 2d)

(6) Expected standard: To answer this question, pupils need to infer that the phrase *'Ah, but weren't Romulus and Remus the sons of Mars, the descendants of Aeneas?'* suggests that no harm would come to the twins.

Pupils need to copy the quotation in full for this question.   **1 mark** (Content Domain 2d)

(7) **Expected standard:** In this question, pupils are asked to make links between the words chosen by the author and how they enhance the idea of a siege. This question also relies on an understanding of Mars's role as the God of War. Pupils should refer to the sentence: 'He *blasted* her with love, *bombarded* her with tender words, *shot* her full of passion.'

Accept answers which list the words *blasted*, *bombarded* and *shot* without copying out the sentence. Pupils should include all three words in their response. **1 mark** (Content Domain 2g)

Extension: In answering why the author chose to use this language when writing about Mars, pupils need to explain that Mars was the God of War and so the use of combative language is reflective of his warlike characteristics. **1 additional mark** (Content Domain 2g)

(8) **Expected standard:** Pupils should explain how the word '*brawling*' suggests that the twins argued and fought with each other. This question relies on an understanding of vocabulary as well as recognising that the author has chosen the word to enhance our understanding of the characters. (The twins' tendency to fight each other is significant in the resolution of the story.) **1 mark** (Content Domain 2g)

(9) **Expected standard:** This question requires pupils to understand the word '*villainous*'. If answering 'yes', they need to infer which of Mars's actions could be interpreted as villainous. Evidence could include:
*   He wooed Rhea Silvia despite knowing the promise she had made.
*   He could have released Rhea Silvia from her tomb, but he had moved on.

If answering 'no', pupils may point to the presence of the wolf and the woodpecker, which suggests that Mars was protecting Romulus and Remus. **1 mark** (Content Domain 2d)

(10) **Expected standard:** In answering this question, pupils are required to gather evidence from across the text. They then need to infer how different characters' actions could be interpreted. Pupils should locate two examples from this list:
*   They were brought into the world as a consequence of the actions of Mars and Rhea Silvia.
*   They were ordered to be drowned by their grandparents.
*   They were saved from drowning by the servants who left them at the edge of the river instead of drowning them in the middle.
*   They were rescued from starvation by the wolf who took them to her den and suckled them.
*   They were brought up by the herdsman and his wife who should have taken them to the authorities. **Up to 2 marks** (Content Domain 2d)

When Hitler Stole Pink Rabbit

Outside the sky was blue and she saw that the people in the street below were not wearing overcoats. There was a lady selling tulips at a stall on the opposite pavement and a chestnut tree at the corner was in full leaf. It was spring. She was amazed how much everything had changed during her illness. The people in the street seemed pleased with the spring weather too and several bought flowers from the stall. The lady selling tulips was round and dark-haired and looked a little bit like Heimpi.

Suddenly Anna remembered something. Heimpi had been going to join them two weeks after they left Germany. Now it must be more than a month. Why hadn't she come? She was going to ask Mama, but Max came in first.

"Max," said Anna, "why hasn't Heimpi come?"

Max looked taken aback. "Do you want to go back to bed?" he said.

"No," said Anna.

"Well," said Max, "I don't know if I'm meant to tell you, but quite a lot happened while you were ill."

"What?" asked Anna.

"You know Hitler won the elections," said Max. "Well, he very quickly took over the whole government, and it's just as Papa said it would be – nobody's allowed to say a word against him. If they do they're thrown into jail."

"Did Heimpi say anything against Hitler?" asked Anna with a vision of Heimpi in a dungeon.

"No, of course not," said Max. "But Papa did. He still does. And so of course no one in Germany is allowed to print anything he writes. So he can't earn any money and we can't afford to pay Heimpi any wages."

"I see," said Anna, and after a moment she added, "are we poor, then?"

"I think we are, a bit," said Max. "Only Papa is going to try to write for some Swiss papers instead – then we'll be all right again." He got up as though to go and Anna said quickly, "I wouldn't have thought Heimpi would mind about money. If we had a little house I think she'd want to come and look after us anyway, even if we couldn't pay her much."

"Yes, well, that's another thing," said Max. He hesitated before he added, "We can't get a house because we haven't any furniture."

"But …" said Anna.

"The Nazis have pinched the lot," said Max. "It's called confiscation of property. Papa had a letter last week." He grinned. "It's been rather like one of those awful plays where people keep rushing in with bad news. And on top of it all there were you, just about to kick the bucket …"

"I wasn't going to kick the bucket!" said Anna indignantly.

"Well, I knew you weren't, of course," said Max, "but that Swiss doctor has a very gloomy imagination. Do you want to go back to bed now?"

"I think I do," said Anna. She was feeling rather weak and Max helped her across the room. When she was safely back in bed she said, "Max, this … confiscation of property, whatever it's called – did the Nazis take everything – even our things?"

Max nodded.

Anna tried to imagine it. The piano was gone … the dining-room curtains with the flowers … her bed … all her toys which included her stuffed Pink Rabbit. For a moment she felt terribly sad about Pink Rabbit. It had had embroidered black eyes – the original glass ones had fallen out years before – and an endearing habit of collapsing on its paws. Its fur, though no longer very pink, had been soft and familiar. How could she ever have chosen to pack that characterless woolly dog in its stead? It had been a terrible mistake, and now she would never be able to put it right.

"I always knew we should have brought the games compendium," said Max. "Hitler's probably playing Snakes and Ladders with it this very minute."

"And snuggling my Pink Rabbit!" said Anna and laughed. But some tears had come into her eyes and were running down her cheeks all at the same time.

"Oh well, we're lucky to be here at all," said Max.

"What do you mean?" asked Anna.

Max looked carefully past her out of the window.

"Papa heard from Heimpi," he said with elaborate casual-ness. "The Nazis came for all our passports the morning after the elections."

When Hitler Stole Pink Rabbit by Judith Kerr

Questions

1 Which of the following are synonyms of 'confiscation'?

restoration   taking away   seizure   impounding   [1 mark]

2 What do we learn about Anna's toy rabbit? Find **three** examples.   [1 mark]

3 Decide whether each statement about the extract is true or false.   [1 mark]

	True	False
Anna had been ill for about one month.		
Heimpi has been thrown into a dungeon by the Nazis.		
The family's housekeeper was left behind in Germany.		
The Nazis have seized the family's property.		

4 Read the first paragraph. Which word indicates that Anna is looking at the scene from an upstairs window?   [1 mark]

5 Which phrase tells us that the family and their doctor thought that Anna was going to die?   [1 mark]

6 How does the phrase 'the people in the street below were not wearing overcoats' enhance the author's description of the weather?   [1 mark]

7 Why do you think Max suggested that Anna might want to go back to bed when she asked why Heimpi had not joined the family?   [2 marks]

8 What job does Anna's father do?   [1 mark]

9 Which word or phrase suggests that Max is trying to remain cheerful whilst telling Anna about the confiscation of the family's property?   [1 mark]

10 When describing the confiscated items, the author gives little detail about the piano and the curtains but a longer description of Pink Rabbit. Why do you think she does this?   [2 marks]

Teaching assessment

1 taking away, seizure, impounding   **1 mark for all three correct** (Content Domain 2a)

2 Pupils should choose from:
- It was stuffed;
- It had embroidered black eyes;
- The original glass eyes had fallen out;
- It had a habit of collapsing on its paws;
- Its fur was no longer pink but was soft and familiar.

Pupils may write in their own words or quote exactly from the text.

1 mark for three correct examples (Content Domain 2b)

3

	True	False
Anna had been ill for about one month.	✓	
Heimpi has been thrown into a dungeon by the Nazis.		✓
The family's housekeeper was left behind in Germany.	✓	
The Nazis have seized the family's property.	✓	

1 mark for all four correct (Content Domain 2c)

4 **Expected standard:** Pupils should write 'below'. This question asks them to infer that 'people in the street below' shows that she was looking from above.   **1 mark** (Content Domain 2d)

5 **Expected standard:** To answer this question, pupils need to understand idiomatic language. Pupils should write the phrase 'kick the bucket'.   **1 mark** (Content Domain 2d)

6 **Expected standard:** Pupils should infer that if people were not wearing overcoats then the weather must be warm. This enhances the description of the spring-like weather without explicitly telling the reader that it was warm.   **1 mark** (Content Domain 2g)

(7) **Expected standard:** To answer this question, pupils need to infer that Max is concerned that the news about Heimpi will upset Anna and that this may cause her to relapse after her long illness.

1 mark (Content Domain 2d)

Extension: Some pupils may be able to refer to the later point in the text where Anna needed to return to bed as she was rather weak as evidence that Max was right that the anguish of what had happened has made her feel ill again.

1 additional mark (Content Domain 2d)

(8) **Expected standard:** Pupils should infer that Anna's father is a newspaper journalist (accept, he is a writer, or he writes for a living). This question requires pupils to infer based on information given at various points across the text.   **1 mark** (Content Domain 2d)

(9) **Expected standard:** Pupils should write *'grinned'* or *'He grinned'*. To answer this question, pupils need to activate their understanding of the word 'grin' as a synonym for smile and so infer that he is smiling and trying to keep cheerful about the situation.

1 mark (Content Domain 2d)

(10) **Expected standard:** Pupils should explain that Pink Rabbit is precious to Anna as it had been her cherished toy. They should explain that by describing it in detail the author draws our attention to just how well Anna knew the toy and how very much she loved it in comparison to the piano and curtains.   **Up to 2 marks** (Content Domain 2g)

The Purple Lady

If something precious is lost, then the search must never end until it is found. But sometimes it means paying a high price to win back what has been taken away.

The last of the snow was brown and sludgy; spindly branches clawed an ice-blue sky; nameless birds crouched silently in black silhouette on naked branches, and the air was drifting with crystals. He rubbed a small circle on the steamy, grimy window through which he could observe this alien world. His search had begun.

Abu had caught the bus to the city.

'Where do you want to get off?' the bus driver had demanded.

Abu didn't know what to say. 'At the end of the line,' he replied finally, and sat at the back by himself. He noticed that whereas his fellow passengers had at first looked out greedily at the new spring-green countryside as if they would never see it again, when they reached the outskirts of the city, with its chimneys, factories and apartment blocks, its roads seething with traffic, they now slumped back wearily, as if dreading their day at work.

A head-scarved woman got on and sat next to Abu as the bus churned along a busy avenue. The pavement streamed with people bundled up in bulky coats, gloves and boots of greys and browns, like the detritus of a slow-moving muddy river.

A figure in purple caught his eye; an indeterminate blur at first – visible, then invisible among the heaving throng, rising and falling as if riding on the crest of a wave, coming closer. It could have been a mystical animal from a bestiary, for there was nothing but the swirl of a cloak of purple fur which enveloped the figure from head to foot, the face lost in the secretive depths of a hood. If anyone on the bus noticed, they didn't show it. On the contrary, they dropped their gaze; some put on dark glasses, turned their heads away from the windows, and huddled closer together as if in earnest conversation. Most of all, they held their children tight.

Behind the figure, a pack of wild dogs broke up the rhythm of the crowds; grey wolf-like forms threaded their predatory way along the pavement like bodyguards and stopped in front of some tall, purple iron-wrought gates.

The figure paused, motionless, staring through the railings, its purple cloak quivering as if, like an alert animal, its fur was about to stand on end.

Abu couldn't see anything on the other side; only a swirling mist that shrouded everything, but as the bus edged forward Abu turned his head and saw a woman's hand emerge from the cloak. A thin grey hound wound about her knees like a serpent. Briefly, she tossed back her head, and he was sure he heard a thin animal-like howl. Then both woman and hound were on the other side of the locked gates, as if, like a coil of mist, they had simply slipped through the bars.

The bus moved on.

'What is that place?' Abu whispered to the woman next to him, who clutched a basket on her knees.

She bowed her head, and looked steadfastly at her bony fingers clutching her basket. 'You shouldn't ask; you shouldn't look,' she muttered. 'Don't you know what happens to anyone who catches the eye of the Purple Lady? Even to look into the eyes of her hounds is to be damned.'

'You mean these are the gates to the kingdom of the Purple Lady?'

'Ssssh!' The woman shuddered. 'You should never take this route into town. It is a cursed place. My daughter was kidnapped by the Purple Lady. Every week I take this bus, and hope that maybe one day I'll see her again. But I'm a coward,' she wept. 'Every time we near those dreadful gates, I dare not look. Yet I know my daughter is somewhere inside those grounds. All of us on this bus have lost someone. See? None of them is looking.'

Abu glanced around: one lady had drawn her veil across her eyes, a man buried his face in his scarf, and another held up a newspaper so that it touched his nose.

Abu felt his body go hot and cold in turn with terror and excitement. So it was true: there *was* a Purple Lady, and this was where she lived. Had he at last found the place where his sister Leyla was being held prisoner?

'The Purple Lady' from *Blackberry Blue and other Fairy Tales* by Jamila Gavin

Questions

1. Which of these words is **not** a synonym of *'detritus'*?

rubbish   wreckage   junk   dregs   booty   *[1 mark]*

2. Choose the correct definition for the word *'bestiary'*.   *[1 mark]*

		Tick one
A	A list of objects or categories with the 'best' at the top of the list.	
B	A hutch or cage for beasts; like an aviary for birds.	
C	An illustrated book about animals, birds and mythical animals.	

3. Write down **two** things you are told about the weather in the text.   *[1 mark]*

4. What does the phrase *'observe this alien world'* suggest about Abu?   *[1 mark]*

5. How can you tell that the bus journey is taking place in the morning?   *[1 mark]*

6. What do you think the connection is between the passengers on the bus and the passage written in italics at the start of the story?   *[3 marks]*

7. How do you think the story will end?   *[3 marks]*

8. In what ways did the people on the bus avoid the gaze of the Purple Lady? Give at least **four** examples.   *[1 mark]*

9. Why do you think the author chose to use the word *'shrouded'* to describe the mist at the Purple Lady's gates?   *[3 marks]*

Teaching assessment

(1) booty **1 mark** (Content Domain 2a)

(2)

		Tick one
A	A list of objects or categories with the 'best' at the top of the list.	
B	A hutch or cage for beasts; like an aviary for birds.	
C	An illustrated book about animals, birds and mythical animals.	✓

1 mark (Content Domain 2a)

(3) Pupils should retrieve two pieces of information about the weather from:
- The snow was brown and sludgy;
- There was an ice-blue sky;
- The air was drifting with crystals. **1 mark** (Content Domain 2b)

(4) **Expected standard:** This question requires pupils to activate their understanding of the word 'alien'. They should then infer that the use of *'alien world'* suggests that the location is unfamiliar or foreign to Abu. It suggests that he has just arrived. Accept answers which refer to Abu coming from another place or country. **1 mark** (Content Domain 2d)

(5) **Expected standard:** Pupils should refer to the phrase *'as if dreading their day at work'* as suggestive of people making their early morning commute. **1 mark** (Content Domain 2d)

(6) **Expected standard:** To answer this question, pupils are required to consider the text as a whole and reflect on how the introduction may hold meaning for the rest of the story. They are also required to infer what could be meant by the word *'precious'* in the story. Pupils will need to show the connection between the information shared by the lady with the head-scarf about her daughter and the introductory section which discusses the need to search for precious things that have been lost. In their answers, pupils will need to explain that children are precious to their parents and that the people on the bus have lost their children or other loved ones. **Up to 2 marks** (Content Domain 2f)

Extension: Some pupils may infer that the introductory section works as a summary of the story. **1 additional mark** (Content Domain 2f)

(7) **Expected standard:** Any reasonable answer based on information stated and implied in the text should be accepted. Award 1 mark for responses with single pieces of evidence from the text. E.g. *I think Abu will go on a quest to find his sister and get her back from the Purple Lady.* **1 mark** (Content Domain 2e)

Extension: Some pupils will provide fully developed answers which refer to more than one point in the story. E.g. *I think the Purple Lady has taken Abu's sister. I think he will go on a quest to find her and get her back. As all the other people on the bus have lost people, I think Abu will get them back too. I think the introduction is important. The lost children are the precious things that have been lost, which is why Abu will go and look for them. He will succeed as it's a fairy tale but I think he will suffer a high price in the process. After all, this is what the introduction to the story says.* **Up to 2 additional marks** (Content Domain 2e)

8 Pupils should retrieve at least four answers from the text. This question requires them to know synonyms for *'gaze'* and to be able to interpret that some actions are inferred, such as avoiding looking at the Purple Lady. Information is located at two points in the text.
Pupils should retrieve four of the following:

- they dropped their gaze;
- some put on dark glasses;
- turned their heads away from the windows;
- huddled closer together as if in earnest conversation;
- one lady had drawn her veil across her eyes;
- a man buried his face in his scarf;
- and another man held up a newspaper so that it touched his nose.

1 mark (Content Domain 2b)

9 **Expected standard:** This question requires pupils to know the meaning of the word *'shrouded'* as something that hides or conceals from view and to explain that this is what the mist is doing. **1 mark** (Content Domain 2g)

Extension: Some pupils may be able to explain how the mist shrouding the view increases the mystery and tension in the scene as Abu doesn't yet know what is behind the gates or who he is looking at. Some pupils may also refer to connotations of death, as a shroud is used to cover a body for burial. They should explain that this adds an additional sinister note to the use of *'shrouded'*. **Up to 2 additional marks** (Content Domain 2g)

I am Malala

Day or night, my father's courage never seemed to waiver, despite receiving threatening letters as well as advice from concerned friends. As the school bombings continued, he spoke out against them; he even went to the site of one school bombing while it was still a smouldering wreck. And he went back and forth to Islamabad and Peshawar, pleading with the government for help and speaking out against the Taliban.

I could see that my mother was worried at times. She would hug us close and pray over us before we left for school and as soon as we came home. And she sat late into the night with her phone in her hand – trying not to call my father every hour.

She talked to us of plans for what we would do if the Taliban came. She thought she could sleep with a knife under her pillow. I said I could sneak into the toilet and call the police. I thought of the magic pencil I used to pray for. Now would be as good a time as any for my prayer to finally be answered.

Back at school my friends and I wondered what we could do. So Madam Maryam and my father worked with us on essays and speeches in which we expressed our feelings about the Taliban's campaign to destroy girls' schools and about how much our own school meant to us. We planned an assembly where we would make our speeches; we called it a peace rally but it was just going to be a handful of us upper-school girls.

The day of the assembly, a Pashto TV crew arrived at our school. We were excited and surprised – we didn't think anyone would care what a group of girls had to say about peace. Some girls were nervous, but I had given a few interviews by this time, and I was a bit more comfortable in front of a camera, although, truth be told, I did still get nervous.

We were a democracy at the Khushal School so every girl would get a chance to speak. The older girls went first. They talked about our friends who had quit school out of fear. They talked about how much we loved to learn.

Then it was Moniba's turn. Moniba, our public-speaking champion, stepped to the front and spoke like a poet. 'We Pashtuns are a religion-loving people,' she said. 'Because of the Taliban, the whole world is claiming we are terrorists. This is not the case. We are peace-loving. Our mountains, our trees, our flowers – everything in our valley is about peace.'

After Moniba spoke, it was my turn. My mouth was as dry as dust. I was anxious, as I often was before interviews, but I knew this was an important opportunity to spread our message of peace and education. As soon as they put a microphone in front of me, the words came out – sure and steady, strong and proud. 'This is not the Stone Age,' I said. 'But it feels like we are going backwards. Girls are getting more deprived of our rights.' I spoke about how much I loved school. About how important it was to keep learning. 'We are afraid of no one, and we will continue our education. This is our dream.' And I knew in that instant that it wasn't me, Malala, speaking; my voice was the voice of so many others who wanted to speak but couldn't.

Microphones made me feel as if I was speaking to the whole world. I had only talked to local TV stations and newspapers, but still, I felt as if the wind would carry my words, the same way it scatters flower pollen in the spring, planting seeds all over the earth.

And I had started a funny habit: I sometimes found myself looking in the mirror and giving speeches.

Our house was often full of relatives from Shangla who came to Mingora when they needed to go to the doctor or do some shopping. The kitchen was full of aunties gossiping. The guest room was full of uncles arguing. And the house was full of little children playing. And crying. And arguing. With all this chaos swirling about, I would escape into the bathroom and look in the mirror. When I looked in the mirror though, I didn't see myself. I saw hundreds of people listening to me.

My mother's voice would snap me out of my daydream. '*Pisho*,'* she'd say. 'What are you doing in there? Our guests need to use the bathroom.'

I felt quite silly sometimes, when I realised I was giving a speech to a mirror in the toilet. 'Malala,' I would say to myself, 'what are you doing?'

Maybe, I thought, I was still that little Malala who lectured an empty classroom.

But maybe it was something more. Maybe that girl in the mirror, that girl who imagined speaking to the world, was the Malala I would become. So throughout 2008, as our Swat** was being attacked, I didn't stay silent. I spoke to local and national TV channels, radio and newspapers – I spoke out to anyone who would listen.

*Pisho = cat, kitten
**Swat = the valley where Malala's hometown was situated

I am Malala by Malala Yousafzai with Patricia McCormick

Questions

1 Which of the following are synonyms of *'rally'*?

gathering   separation   dispersal   assembly   meeting   *[1 mark]*

2 What was the name of the city where Malala lived?   *[1 mark]*

3 In what ways did Malala's mother show her anxiety? Write down **three** examples.   *[1 mark]*

4 Decide whether each statement about the extract is true or false.   *[1 mark]*

	True	**False**
Terrorists were destroying schools across the country.		
Malala spent time looking at her reflection and admiring her appearance.		
The arrival of a TV crew caused the girls to abandon their peace rally.		
As a democracy, all the girls had a turn at presenting their opinions.		

5 How can you tell that everyone in Malala's school had equal rights?   *[3 marks]*

6 Malala was proud of Moniba. Find **two** examples from the text to support this opinion.   *[1 mark]*

7 What feeling does Malala convey when she tells the reader that her *'mouth was as dry as dust'*?   *[1 mark]*

8 *'And I knew in that instant that it wasn't me, Malala, speaking; my voice was the voice of so many others who wanted to speak but couldn't.'*

Who are the others that Malala refers to here?   *[1 mark]*

9 Malala refers to her words as flower pollen being scattered by the wind. What do you think she wants to happen with her words?   *[1 mark]*

10 *'With all this chaos swirling about, I would escape into the bathroom and look in the mirror.'*

What is the impression created by Malala's use of *'escape'* in this phrase?   *[1 mark]*

Teaching assessment

Supporting pupils to read and understand non-fiction

When answering questions about non-fiction, encourage pupils to read the extract all the way through first. Encourage them to think about why the text has been written. Is it trying to inform, describe, persuade or give instructions? Pupils should also consider whether the information contained in the text is objective or shows bias. Pupils are now ready to think about how the writer has used features to organise the text. In looking at language, pupils should underline any important vocabulary and put a circle around any words they are unsure about. They may be able to work out what these mean from the context. Pupils are now ready to start answering questions about the text.

(1) gathering, assembly, meeting **1 mark for all three correct** (Content Domain 2a)

(2) Mingora **1 mark** (Content Domain 2b)

(3) Pupils should select three examples from the following list:
- Hugging the children close to her;
- Praying over them;
- Sitting up late trying not to call Malala's father every hour;
- Making plans for if the Taliban came, such as sleeping with a knife under her pillow.

1 mark for three examples (Content Domain 2b)

(4)

	True	False
Terrorists were destroying schools across the country.	✓	
Malala spent time looking at her reflection and admiring her appearance.		✓
The arrival of a TV crew caused the girls to abandon their peace rally.		✓
As a democracy, all the girls had a turn at presenting their opinions.	✓	

1 mark for all four correct (Content Domain 2c)

(5) **Expected standard:** To answer this question, pupils need to understand the word 'democracy'. E.g. *Malala described the Khushal School as a democracy; this means that everyone had equal rights.* **1 mark** (Content Domain 2d)

Extension: In addition to explaining the meaning of democracy, some pupils may also refer to the phrase: *'every girl would get a chance to* speak' within their answers. E.g. *Malala described the Khushal School as a democracy, which means that everyone had equal rights. She goes on to say that they all had a chance to speak, which is a sign of their democracy.* **2 additional marks** (Content Domain 2d)

(6) **Expected standard:** Pupils should refer to the phrases *'our public-speaking champion'* and *'spoke like a poet'* as evidence of Malala's pride in Moniba. **1 mark** (Content Domain 2d)

(7) **Expected standard:** Pupils should explain that Malala conveys feelings of nervousness or anxiety through her use of *'mouth was as dry as dust'*. This question requires pupils to understand how Malala's use of figurative language enhances her description of her anxiety at this point of the narrative. **1 mark** (Content Domain 2g)

(8) **Expected standard:** Pupils should be able to infer that Malala is referring to the other girls in Pakistan who were unable to speak out about the Taliban closing girls' schools. **1 mark** (Content Domain 2d)

(9) **Expected standard:** Pupils should be able to infer that the *'flower pollen'* in this simile refers to Malala's words. They should then explain that she wanted her words to travel around the world and to germinate, as pollen does. **1 mark** (Content Domain 2e)

(10) **Expected standard:** Pupils should be able to identify that by using the word 'escape' Malala creates an impression that she needed to get away from her family at this point of the narrative, and find the space to be on her own. Earlier in the quotation she uses the phrase *'chaos swirling about'* which clearly denotes that it was busy and noisy in the house. When she went to the bathroom she was on her own and so we can assume it was quiet and more orderly than the rest of the house. **1 mark** (Content Domain 2g)

The Visitor

A crumbling churchyard, the sea and the moon;

The waves had gouged out grave and bone;

A man was walking, late and alone…

He saw a skeleton on the ground;

A ring on a bony finger he found.

He ran home to his wife and gave her the ring.

'Oh, where did you get it?' He said not a thing.

'It's the loveliest ring in the world,' she said,

As it glowed on her finger. They slipped off to bed.

At midnight they woke. In the dark outside,

'Give me my ring!' a chill voice cried.

'What was that, William? What did it say?'

'Don't worry, my dear. It'll soon go away.'

'I'm coming!' A skeleton opened the door.

'Give me my ring!' It was crossing the floor.

'What was that, William? What did it say?'

'Don't worry, my dear. It'll soon go away.'

'I'm reaching you now! I'm climbing the bed.'

The wife pulled the sheet right over her head.

It was torn from her grasp and tossed in the air.

'I'll drag you out of bed by the hair!'

'What was that, William? What did it say?'

'Throw the ring through the window! THROW IT AWAY!'

She threw it. The skeleton leapt from the sill,

Scooped up the ring and clattered downhill,

Fainter… and fainter… Then all was still.

The Visitor by Ian Serraillier

Questions

(1) List the characters in the poem. [1 mark]

(2) Which of these words is **not** a synonym of 'gouged out'?

scoop out   excavate   hollow out   valley [1 mark]

(3) Summarise the poem in your own words. [2 marks]

(4) What do you notice about the way the poem is organised? [3 marks]

(5) Why has the poet chosen to use capitals for 'THROW IT AWAY'? [1 mark]

(6) How do you think William's wife will react once she's certain the
skeleton has gone? [3 marks]

(7) Compare these lines. What do you notice about the pace of the rhythm? Why do you
think the poet has done this?

A crumbling churchyard, the sea and the moon;
The waves had gouged out grave and bone;
A man was walking, late and alone...

It was torn from her grasp and tossed in the air.
'I'll drag you out of bed by your hair!' [3 marks]

(8) The poem finishes with the word 'still'. What impression does this give you
about the skeleton? [2 marks]

(9) Ellipses are used to create different effects in the first and last stanza.
Explain how they are used. [2 marks]

(10) What evidence suggests the house is at the top of a hill? [1 mark]

Teaching assessment

(1) William, William's wife, the skeleton   **1 mark for all three correct** (Content Domain 2b)

(2) valley   **1 mark** (Content Domain 2a)

(3) Pupils should use their own words to tell the narrative of the poem. Look for key points such as the grave being exposed through the action of the waves, William taking the ring, William avoiding his wife's questioning, the appearance of the skeleton, William's wife asking him three times what the skeleton said, the skeleton's threats, William telling his wife to throw the ring out of the window, William's wife throwing the ring away and the departure of the skeleton.
Up to 2 marks (Content Domain 2c)

(4) **Expected standard:** Pupils should be able to be able to identify that the poem is structured with an opening stanza of three lines and that this is mirrored in the final stanza, also of three lines. They should also be able to identify that the rest of the poem is structured with 10 sets of rhyming couplets.   **1 mark** (Content Domain 2g)

Extension: In addition to the above, some pupils may note the following organisational features. Whilst the opening and closing stanzas are both of three lines, their structures are not identical:
- two lines of the opening stanza rhyme (bone, alone; although some pupils may refer to *'moon'* as a half-rhyme) and all three lines of the final stanza rhyme (*'sill'*, *'downhill'*, *'still'*);
- the first stanza is one sentence separated with semi-colons whilst the final stanza is three separate sentences.   **Up to 2 additional marks** (Content Domain 2g)

(5) **Expected standard:** Pupils should note how the use of capitals reflects William's urgency to be rid of the ring. Some pupils may refer to William's fear of the skeleton, especially after it climbed on the bed.

Whilst the use of capitals indicates that William is shouting, pupils should refer to the fear and urgency that William is feeling. It is not enough to say 'he is shouting'.
1 mark (Content Domain 2g)

(6) **Expected standard:** Pupils should predict the wife's relief that the incident is over. They should refer to the final stanza in supporting this prediction as it implies that all is now calm. *'Fainter…and fainter… Then all was still.'* **1 mark** (Content Domain 2e)

Extension: Pupils may be able to draw on information from across the poem in formulating responses, reflecting the wife's emotional response to what has happened. Credit should be given to responses referring to negative emotions such as anger or disappointment with William for avoiding the truth about the source of the ring. In doing this, pupils should refer to the line *'"Oh, where did you get it?" He said not a thing.'* Pupils may also refer to *'"Give me my ring!" a chill voice cried.'* as further evidence that William had stolen the ring and avoided telling his wife the truth. Pupils may also use the same evidence and predict that the wife feels anger / disappointment / revulsion with William for giving her a dead person's ring. **Up to 2 additional marks** (Content Domain 2e)

(7) **Expected standard:** Pupils should note the contrast in pace and rhythm between the stanzas provided. They should be able to articulate that the first stanza is slow and calm and the second stanza fast and short. They should be able to support their response by referring to the use of long and short syllables in the first stanza and the use of short syllables only in the second stanza. **Up to 2 marks** (Content Domain 2g)

Extension: In discussing the effectiveness of this, pupils may be able to explain how the rhythmic combination of short and long syllables in the opening stanza creates a sense of calm. They should contrast this with the fast rhythm in the second stanza created by short syllables, which reflects the pace of the story and the frightening behaviour of the skeleton. **1 additional mark** (Content Domain 2g)

(8) **Expected standard:** Pupils should refer to the stillness of the bedroom scene now the skeleton has left. Their answers should refer to the implication that the skeleton has returned to its grave and will not be coming back to haunt William and his wife. Some pupils may note that being 'still' is exactly what the skeleton will be, once it is back in its grave. **Up to 2 marks** (Content Domain 2d)

(9) **Expected standard:** Pupils should refer to the way that in the opening stanza the ellipsis is used to introduce the rest of the narrative. In the final stanza they are used to show that the skeleton is getting further and further away from the house. **1 mark** (Content Domain 2g)

Extension: Some pupils may also reflect on the way the ellipses in the final stanza work to slow down the pace of the narrative and so echo the poet's intention of creating a sense of calm and peace after the calamity of the preceding narrative. **1 additional mark** (Content Domain 2g)

(10) The skeleton *'clattered downhill'* suggests that the house is at the top of a hill. **1 mark** (Content Domain 2b)

The Mystery of the Clockwork Sparrow

Her shoulders slumped as she thought of the long week that lay ahead of her, but at once she frowned at herself sharply. Papa would have said that she ought to be thinking about how fortunate she was to be here. There were plenty of others who weren't so lucky, she reminded herself. She had seen them: girls her own age or even younger, selling apples or little posies of flowers on street corners; girls begging for pennies from passing gentlemen; girls huddled in doorways, wearing clothes that were scarcely more than rags.

Thinking this, she shook her head, squared her shoulders and forced herself to smile. 'Buck up,' she told her reflection sternly. Whatever else happened today, she was determined that she wouldn't give Edith any more excuses to call her stuck-up.

She strode purposefully towards the door, but before she had taken more than a couple of steps, she tripped and fell forwards.

'Oh!' exclaimed a voice. As she righted herself, she glanced down to see a boy gazing up at her in alarm. He was sitting on the floor, partly hidden behind a row of coats, and she had fallen over his boots. 'Are you all right?'

'What are you *doing* down there?' demanded Sophie breathlessly, more embarrassed to have been caught pulling faces and talking to herself than actually hurt. No doubt this boy would make fun of her now, like all the rest, and he'd soon be telling all the others what he had overheard. 'You shouldn't hide in corners spying!' she burst out.

'I wasn't spying,' said the boy, scrambling to his feet. He was wearing the Sinclair's porters' uniform – trim dark-blue trousers, a matching jacket with a double row of brass buttons and a peaked hat – but the jacket looked too big for him, the trousers a bit short, and the hat was askew on his untidy, straw-coloured hair. 'I was *reading*.' For proof, he held out a crumpled story-paper, entitled *Boys of Empire*, in one grubby hand.

But before Sophie could say anything else, the door slammed open, and a cluster of shop girls pushed their way into the room, in a flurry of skirts and ribbons.

'Excuse us! Beg your pardon!'

A pretty dark-haired girl caught sight of the boy and smirked. 'Haven't you fetched that tin of elbow grease for Jim yet?' she demanded, sending a ripple of titters through the group.

'Learned to tie your bootlaces all by yourself, have you?' another girl giggled.

A third took in Sophie, and made a ridiculous curtsy in her direction. 'Forgive us, Your Ladyship. We didn't see that you were gracing us with your presence.'

'Aren't you going to introduce us to your young man?' added the dark-haired girl in an arch tone, making the others laugh even more.

The boy's cheeks flushed crimson, but Sophie tried her hardest to look indifferent. She had heard this kind of thing many times already during the two weeks of training that all the Sinclair's shop girls had undertaken. She had realised that she had started all wrong on the very first morning, arriving wearing one of her best dresses – black silk and velvet with jet buttons. She had thought she ought to be smart and make a good first impression, but when she arrived, she realised that every other girl in the room was dressed almost identically, in a plain dark skirt, and a neat white blouse. The rustle and swish of her skirts had made them all look at her, and then begin giggling behind their hands.

'Who does she think she is? The Lady of the Manor?' the dark-haired girl, Edith, had whispered.

The next morning she had come carefully dressed in a navy-blue skirt and a white blouse with a little lace collar, but it was already too late. The girls called her 'Your Ladyship', or if they wanted to be especially mean, 'Your Royal Highness' or 'Princess Sophie'. All through the training, they made game of the way she spoke, the clothes she wore, the way she did her hair, and especially whenever she was praised by Mr Cooper or Claudine, the store window-dresser.

She had tried hard to look unconcerned, and not to let her feelings show. Papa had always said that in times of war, the most important thing was never to let the enemy see that you were intimidated. Remembering this she saw his face again, almost as if he were standing right in front of her with his bright, dark eyes and neat moustache. He would have been pacing up and down on the hearth rug in his study, the walls hung with maps and treasures he had brought back from distant lands, relating one of his many stories about battles and military campaigns. *Keep calm, keep your head, keep a stiff upper lip*: those were his mottoes. But the truth was, the more she ignored the other shop girls, the worse they seemed to become. They said she was haughty and high-and-mighty, and called her the name she hated most, 'Sour-milk Sophie'. Not for the first time, she reflected that perhaps Papa's advice was not *entirely* helpful when it came to dealing with horrid shop girls.

Now, she turned away and went out into the passage, the boy trailing behind her. He looked so miserable that she felt a twinge of guilt for having assumed that he would make fun of her, when, in fact, it seemed that they were in the same boat.

The Mystery of the Clockwork Sparrow by Katherine Woodfine

Questions

1 Match the phrases to their definitions and write them in your book. *[1 mark]*

stiff upper lip	sounding amused because you know more about a situation than other people
buck up	not showing your emotions when in a challenging situation
in an arch tone	encouraging yourself or others to cheer up
high-and-mighty	being in the same difficult circumstances as someone else
in the same boat	behaving as though you're better than other people

2 Write **two** examples of how some girls were less fortunate than Sophie. *[1 mark]*

3 What was Sophie's father's profession? Copy down the word/s or phrases that tell you this. *[1 mark]*

4 What does *'Her shoulders slumped'* suggest about how Sophie felt about her work? *[1 mark]*

5 How do the words *'The boy's cheeks flushed crimson'* help you to understand how he was feeling? *[1 mark]*

6 *'Sophie tried her hardest to look indifferent'* when the shop girls were teasing her and the boy. Find and copy a line from later in the text where she tries to look indifferent again. *[1 mark]*

7 Find and copy **at least three** phrases that show the boy had a dishevelled appearance. *[1 mark]*

8 What evidence is there that Sophie tried to 'fit in' with the other girls on her second day at work? *[3 marks]*

9 What evidence is there that the other girls were jealous of Sophie's upbringing? List **at least three** examples. *[1 mark]*

Teaching assessment

1

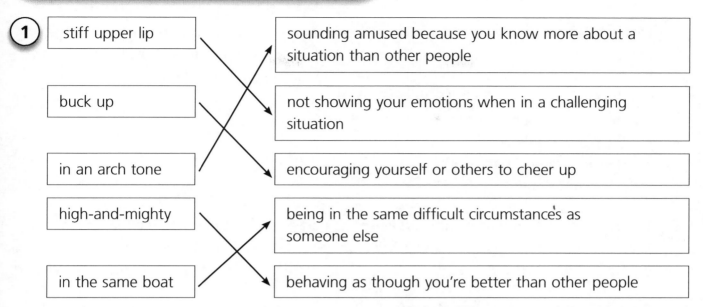

stiff upper lip	sounding amused because you know more about a situation than other people
buck up	not showing your emotions when in a challenging situation
in an arch tone	encouraging yourself or others to cheer up
high-and-mighty	being in the same difficult circumstances as someone else
in the same boat	behaving as though you're better than other people

1 mark for all five correct (Content Domain 2a)

2 Pupils should choose two examples of how the less-fortunate girls were living from:
- selling apples or little posies of flowers on street corners;
- begging for pennies from passing gentlemen;
- girls huddled in doorways, wearing clothes that were scarcely more than rags.

1 mark (Content Domain 2b)

3 Pupils should copy the word/s or phrases that show Sophie's father was a soldier. The question requires pupils to retrieve the relevant information whilst drawing on their knowledge of words associated with the military.
Pupils should refer to the quotation: *'one of his many stories about battles and military campaigns.'*
Accept answers where pupils have written the words 'battles' and 'campaigns' without copying the full quotation. **1 mark** (Content Domain 2b)

4 **Expected standard:** Pupils should be able to infer that Sophie's shoulders slumping indicates that she was feeling unhappy about going to work. This question requires pupils to infer Sophie's emotional state from a statement about her actions. **1 mark** (Content Domain 2d)

5 **Expected standard:** Pupils should explain how the phrase *'The boy's cheeks flushed crimson'* indicates that he was blushing and that this helps show the reader that he was feeling embarrassed. **1 mark** (Content Domain 2g)

6 **Expected standard:** Pupils need to find and copy the line *'She had tried hard to look unconcerned, and not to let her feelings show.'* To answer this question, pupils need to understand what is meant by the word 'indifferent'. **1 mark** (Content Domain 2f)

(7) **Expected standard:** To answer this question, pupils need to know that 'dishevelled' means untidy. They are then required to infer which aspects of his appearance make the boy appear untidy. Pupils should be able to locate three or more of the following phrases:

- the jacket looked too big for him;
- the trousers a bit short;
- the hat was askew;
- untidy, straw-coloured hair;
- one grubby hand.   **1 mark** (Content Domain 2d)

(8) **Expected standard:** Pupils should refer to the part of the text that tells the reader that Sophie wore *'a navy-blue skirt and a white blouse with a little lace collar'* as a way of trying to fit in with the other girls.   **1 mark** (Content Domain 2d)

Extension: Some pupils may also refer back to the previous paragraph where we are told that Sophie had over-dressed for work and that the other girls were almost identical *'in a plain dark skirt, and a neat white blouse.'*   **Up to 2 additional marks** (Content Domain 2d)

(9) **Expected standard:** In answering this question, pupils need to locate information showing that the girls were teasing Sophie for her upper-class habits and characteristics. They will need to infer that these words and phrases indicate envy of her social position. Examples could include:

- curtsying to her;
- calling her Your Ladyship;
- calling her The Lady of the Manor;
- calling her Your Royal Highness;
- calling her Princess Sophie;
- saying she was haughty;
- making a game of the way she spoke and did her hair.   **1 mark** (Content Domain 2d)

Arthur: High King of Britain

I can still see clear in my mind the wild forests of Wales and the wind-blasted mountains above them where I passed my early years. And they were carefree, those years, I had a mother for my best friend, and a father for my constant companion and teacher. He taught me how to hunt, to stalk silently, to kill cleanly. From him I learnt how to handle a hawk, to sweeten in a fox, to hold a bow without a tremble as I pulled it taut, and to use a sword and a spear as a knight should. But from my mother I learnt the great things. I learnt what is right, what is wrong, what should be and what should not be – lessons I am still learning even now, my friend. I never in my life have loved anyone more than my mother, and I think I never hated anyone more than my elder brother Kay.

Kay was six years older than I was and the bane of my young life. Time and again he would foist the blame for his own misdeeds on to my shoulders, for ever trying to turn Father against me – and in this he often succeeded. I would find myself banished to my room or whipped for something I had not done. I can see now the triumphant sneer in my brother's eyes. But with Mother he was never able to taint me. She would never hear a word against me, from Kay or from Father. She was my constant ally, my rock.

But she died. She died when I was just twelve years old. As she lay on her deathbed, her eyes open and unseeing, I reached out to touch her cheek for the last time. Kay grasped my arm and pulled me back.

'Don't you dare touch her,' he said, eyes blazing. 'She's my mother, not yours. You don't have a mother.' I appealed to Father and saw the flicker in his eye that told me that Kay was speaking the truth.

'Kay,' he said, shaking his head sadly. 'How can you say such a thing now, and with your mother lying still warm in death? What I told you, I told you in trust. How can you be so cruel? And you a son of mine.'

'And me?' I said. 'Am I not a son of yours too? Was she not my mother?'

'Neither,' said Father, and he looked away from me. 'I would have told you before, but could never bring myself to do it.'

'Then,' I cried, 'if I am not yours, and if I am not hers, whose am I? I can't be nobody's child.'

He took me by the shoulders. 'Dear boy,' he said, and he suddenly looked an old man, 'I cannot tell you who you are. All I know is that you were brought here as a newborn baby by Merlin. It was Merlin who made me promise to keep you, to protect you and to bring you up as I would my own son and this I have done to my very best. If there have been times when I was hard on you, then it was because I always had that promise to fulfil.'

'Merlin?' I asked. 'Who is this Merlin?'

Kay scoffed at that. 'Do you do nothing but dream? Everyone knows who Merlin is. He's the maker of the old druid magic, a weaver of spells, a soothsayer. He knows what will happen, long before it does happen. He knows everything that has been and everything that will be. Why he bothered with you I can't imagine.'

I turned to Father. 'Is this all true? I was brought here by this Merlin? My mother is not my mother? You are not my father?' He nodded and I could see the pain in his face reflecting my own. But Kay had to rub more salt in the wound.

'So you see,' he crowed. 'You are … a foundling. You should be grateful we took you in.'

At that my blood was up. Small though I was, I felled him with one blow and I would have done him more damage had not Father pulled me off him.

'That is not the way I have taught you, Arthur,' he said, still holding me back. But I broke free of him and ran off into the forest. There I wandered for days and days like some wounded animal, maddened with pain.

Arthur: High King of Britain by Michael Morpurgo

Questions

1 Match each word to its definition and write them in your book. *[1 mark]*

foist		a contemptuous or mocking smile or remark
sneer		being sent away as punishment
triumphant		feeling or expression of having won
banished		to force or impose something upon a person

2 Find and copy the sentence that tells us Merlin was a sorcerer. *[1 mark]*

3 Decide whether each statement about the extract is true or false. *[1 mark]*

	True	False
Arthur's father taught him survival skills.		
Mother taught Arthur how to sew and cook.		
Arthur was unaware of Merlin the sorcerer.		

4 How old was Kay when Mother died? *[1 mark]*

5 '"Don't you dare touch her," he said, eyes blazing.' What does 'eyes blazing' suggest about how Kay is feeling? *[1 mark]*

6 How is the portrayal of Mother and Arthur's relationship enhanced through the use of the word 'ally'? *[1 mark]*

7 How do these phrases improve your understanding of Kay's feelings towards Arthur?
- 'Don't you dare touch her … She's my mother, not yours…'
- 'Do you do nothing but dream? Everyone knows who Merlin is…'
- '"So you see," he crowed. "You are a foundling…"' *[1 mark]*

8 What is the wound Arthur is speaking about when he says 'But Kay had to rub more salt in the wound.'? *[2 marks]*

9 '"Neither," said Father, **and he looked away from me**. "I would have told you before, but could never bring myself to do it."'

What do you infer by Father looking away from Arthur at this point in the story? *[3 marks]*

10 How do you think Arthur's relationship with Kay will develop once Mother has died? Provide evidence from the text to support your opinion. *[1 mark]*

Teaching assessment

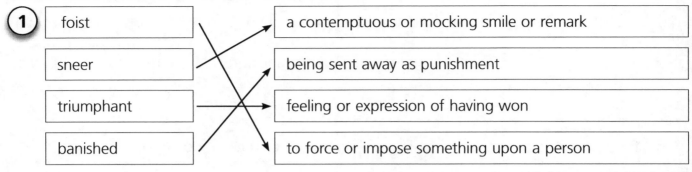

1

foist		a contemptuous or mocking smile or remark
sneer		being sent away as punishment
triumphant		feeling or expression of having won
banished		to force or impose something upon a person

1 mark (Content Domain 2a)

2 To answer this question, pupils need to activate their understanding of vocabulary. They then need to retrieve the sentence telling us that Merlin was a sorcerer: *'He's the maker of the old druid magic, a weaver of spells, a soothsayer.'*   **1 mark** (Content Domain 2b)

3

	True	False
Arthur's father taught him survival skills.	✓	
Mother taught Arthur how to sew and cook.		✓
Arthur was unaware of Merlin the sorcerer.	✓	

1 mark for all three correct (Content Domain 2c)

4 **Expected standard:** To answer this question, pupils need to read across the text to retrieve information telling them that Kay was six years older than Arthur and that Arthur was twelve when Mother died. So Kay was 18.   **1 mark** (Content Domain 2d)

5 **Expected standard:** Pupils need to infer that *'eyes blazing'* suggests that Kay was fiercely angry.   **1 mark** (Content Domain 2d)

6 **Expected standard:** To answer this question, pupils need to understand the meaning of the word *'ally'*. They then need to explain that its use shows how Mother was Arthur's supporter and defender.
Also accept answers that include: working together; they were friends; they helped each other; they were on each other's sides.   **1 mark** (Content Domain 2g)

7 **Expected standard:** Pupils need to explain that the phrases demonstrate how much Kay dislikes or resents Arthur. Some pupils may recognise that the phrases come from across the text and build up a sustained picture of hatred and unkindness.   **1 mark** (Content Domain 2f)

(8) **Expected standard:** To answer this question, pupils need to understand the idiomatic phrase *'rub more salt in the wound'*. They then need to be able to explain that Arthur's wound is the pain of discovering Mother and Father are not his parents.　　**1 mark** (Content Domain 2d)

Extension: Some pupils may be able to explain that rubbing salt in a wound makes it hurt more, and this is what Kay was doing by taunting Arthur that he was a foundling.

1 additional mark (Content Domain 2d)

(9) **Expected standard:** To answer this question, pupils need to infer that the words *'and he looked away from me'* indicate that Father was unable to make eye-contact with Arthur.

1 mark (Content Domain 2d)

Extension: Some pupils may be able to explain that avoiding eye-contact is often associated with feelings of shame or guilt. This explanation is further enhanced by Father saying *'I would have told you before, but could never bring myself to do it.'*

Up to 2 additional marks (Content Domain 2d)

(10) **Expected standard:** Accept any reasonable answer supported by evidence from the text. E.g. *I think Kay will continue to get Arthur in trouble with Father because he had often succeeded in the past. Only now that Mother is dead, he is without his constant ally so will get into more trouble and feel much more alone.*　　**1 mark** (Content Domain 2e)

The Cloudspotter's Guide

So what exactly is a Cumulus cloud? It may feel rather unsatisfying to hear that it is just water. And yet, like all clouds, that is all it is. The curious cloudspotter might therefore wonder why it looks so different from a glass of the stuff down here on the ground. The cloud's white, opaque appearance is because the water is in the form of countless tiny droplets (well, around 10,000,000,000 per cubic metre in actual fact), each only a few thousandths of a millimetre across. And this array of innumerable tiny surfaces scatters the light in all directions, giving the cloud its diffuse, milky appearance as compared with the single surface of a container of water. It is like the rough face of etched glass compared with a smooth pane: all the minute angled surfaces of the roughened glass make it look white as they scatter the light every which way.

According to ancient Hindu and Buddhist beliefs Cumulus clouds are the spiritual cousins of elephants, which is why the animals are worshipped, with a view to bringing rain after India's scorching summer heat. 'Megha', meaning cloud in classical Hindi, is the name used to address elephants in these prayers. The Sanskrit creation myths describe how elephants created at the beginning of time were white, had wings to fly, could change their shape at will and had the power to bring rain. Although they have now lost these magical powers, the present-day descendants of those early Uber-elephants are still believed to have an affinity with the clouds – especially the albino ones.

It is somewhat alarming to learn that eighty elephants weigh about as much as the water droplets in a medium-sized Cumulus – a Cumulus mediocris – would if you added them all together.* For, though the droplets in a Cumulus cloud are extremely small, there are one hell of a lot of them. Given that elephants don't tend to fly these days, how exactly does the water equivalent of eighty of them rise to form a Cumulus?

There's a clue in the cloud's tendency to appear on a sunny day. For when the Sun is shining, currents of air known as thermals, or convection currents, start to form as it warms the ground. These rising plumes of air are the light turbulence you feel as you pass through Cumulus in an aeroplane. They are the reason why hang gliders and eagles will head towards this type of cloud, knowing that it is a celestial signpost for the updraughts that give them lift. Thermals are the invisible spirits that give life to the Cumulus. They bring it into being, flowing through it, animating it.

To understand the formation of thermal convection currents is to glimpse the soul of a Cumulus cloud. They are what get the moisture up there in the first place and also what help the cloud's droplets to stay airborne for the ten minutes or so of a typical Cumulus's life.

It's a lot like the movement of the blobs of oil in a lava lamp. The mixture of oil and coloured water inside the lamp moves upwards by the same process of convection as air on a sunny day. Although the lamp contains liquids rather than gases, the principle is the same.

The oil in the lamp is normally just a bit denser than the water, and so sits at the bottom, but when the bulb in the base warms it up, the oil expands, becomes a little less dense, and begins to float up lazily through the water. The air outside behaves in a similar way. A ploughed field that has been warmed by the Sun can act like the bulb in the lamp, warming the air above – making it expand, become less dense and float upwards through the surrounding cooler air. The invisible moisture carried in the rising thermal is what can end up as Cumulus, or, in the words of the American poet Maria White Lowell, 'little tender sheep, pastured in fields of blue … with new-shorn fleeces white'.

Remember that Cumulus are individual clouds, quite different from the large layers you see in an overcast sky. For it so happens that some surfaces absorb and give off the Sun's heat better than others, and thus a pocket of air will rise by convection more readily over here than one over there. Tarmac, for instance, will heat the air more efficiently than a grass field. A hillside facing the Sun will do so faster than one in shadow. Cloudspotters will be pleased to see this most clearly demonstrated when sailing around a small island on a sunny day. The surface of the island is warmed by the Sun's radiation more readily than the sea around it, and a puffy, white Cumulus cloud can often be poised above it, fed by the thermal coming off the ground. South Sea Islanders would use Cumulus clouds as beacons, navigating towards an atoll well before the land itself became visible.

Since they form on top of these independent convection currents, Cumulus are separate, individual clouds. This is one of the main ways in which they differ in appearance from other cloud types. Each is the visible summit of a towering transparent column of air – like a bright white toupee on a huge invisible man. And the Cumulus can soon drift off from its thermal host – the wig plucked from his head, swirling and folding in on itself in slow motion as it is swept along in the breeze.

*This is assuming the cloud occupies one cubic kilometre (about 0.24 cubic miles), which is not particularly large for a Cumulus. The droplets will commonly have a combined weight of 2,000,000 kg. The average Asian elephant weighs 2,500 kg.

The Cloudspotter's Guide by Gavin Pretor-Pinney

Questions

1. Find and copy **one** word in paragraph four that means **both** 'positioned in the sky' **and** 'belonging to heaven'. [1 mark]

2. How many elephants have the equivalent weight of a Cumulus mediocris? [1 mark]

3. In which types of weather do Cumulus clouds tend to form? [1 mark]

4. Why do Cumulus clouds tend to form over small islands? [1 mark]

5. Copy the paragraph headings into your book and match to the correct paragraph number. [1 mark]

Heading	Paragraph number
The creation mythology of Cumulus clouds	4
Why eagles and hang gliders head for the clouds	1
Oil, air and water	6
What is a Cumulus cloud?	8
How Cumulus clouds act like signposts over islands	2

6. Explain why albino elephants are believed to have 'an affinity with the clouds'. [2 marks]

7. What do these phrases suggest about the author's beliefs about clouds?
   - invisible spirits that give life…
   - bring it into being…
   - glimpse the soul… [3 marks]

8. Explain how 'little tender sheep, pastured in fields of blue … with new-shorn fleeces white' relates to the image of Cumulus clouds. [3 marks]

9. What is the similarity between 'toupee' and 'summit'? How does this help the reader understand Cumulus clouds? [3 marks]

Teaching assessment

1 'Celestial' means both 'positioned in the sky' and 'belonging to heaven'.

1 mark (Content Domain 2a)

2 About 80 elephants have the equivalent weight of a Cumulus mediocris.

1 mark (Content Domain 2b)

3 Cumulus clouds tend to form on sunny days (accept in sunny weather).

1 mark (Content Domain 2b)

4 To answer this retrieval question, pupils need to find the place in the text that explains how *'The surface of the island is warmed by the Sun's radiation more readily than the sea around it…'* Accept answers in their own words. E.g. *The surface of an island is warmed by the Sun more easily than the sea around it.*   **1 mark** (Content Domain 2b)

5 The paragraph headings and paragraph numbers correlate as follows:

Heading	Paragraph number
The creation mythology of Cumulus clouds	2
Why eagles and hang gliders head for the clouds	4
Oil, air and water	6
What is a Cumulus cloud?	1
How Cumulus clouds act like signposts over islands	8

1 mark for all five correct (Content Domain 2c)

6 **Expected standard:** This question requires pupils to know that animals with albino characteristics are colourless or white. From this, they need to draw on the information given about the mythical white elephants of the Sanskrit creation myth. They should then use this to infer that this is why albino elephants are believed to have an affinity with the clouds. E.g. *Albino elephants are white. In the Sanskrit creation myth elephants could fly and were able to bring the rain. These elephants were white like the clouds. This is where the connection with albino elephants comes from and why they are believed to have an affinity with the clouds.*

Up to 2 marks (Content Domain 2d)

(7) **Expected standard:** To answer this question, pupils need to activate their understanding of vocabulary to explain how the use of *'spirits that give life'*, *'being'* and *'soul'* suggest that the clouds are life-like. Some pupils may describe this as the clouds 'having a life'.

1 mark (Content Domain 2d)

Extension: Some pupils may be able to identify that the author has used personification in giving *'life'*, *'being'* and *'soul'* to the clouds. And that by doing this, he is bringing them alive and giving them human characteristics. Some of these pupils may be able to refer to the spiritual nature of the language chosen by the author. He seems not only to be discussing the 'life' of the clouds but also suggesting a 'spirituality' linked to them. Some pupils may also refer to the author's words at the end of the section where he says *'a typical Cumulus's life'* as part of their explanation. **Up to 2 additional marks** (Content Domain 2d)

(8) **Expected standard:** Pupils should explain how the description *'little tender sheep, pastured in fields of blue … with new-shorn fleeces white'* helps the reader visualise Cumulus clouds as being like white and fluffy sheep, but instead of being in green fields filled with grass, the clouds are found in the blue sky. **1 mark** (Content Domain 2g)

Extension: Some pupils may be able to explain that the quotation is a direct metaphor. The clouds are the white shorn sheep and the field is the blue sky. Some pupils may further explain that as Cumulus clouds tend to form on sunny days with clear blue skies the allusion to blue fields is particularly effective. **Up to 2 additional marks** (Content Domain 2g)

(9) **Expected standard:** This question requires pupils to draw on their knowledge of vocabulary to know the meaning of both *'toupee'* and *'summit'*. The question then requires that they infer that both of these words refer to being on top of something (a head and a mountain respectively). **Up to 2 marks** (Content Domain 2g)

Extension: Some pupils may be able to further say that by making this analogy the author has made clear that Cumulus clouds are more than the cloud itself as there is the column of air underneath, just like there is a body and head beneath a toupee.

1 additional mark (Content Domain 2g)

Five Children and It

The house was three miles from the station, but, before the dusty hired hack had rattled along for five minutes, the children began to put their heads out of the carriage window and say, "Aren't we nearly there?" And every time they passed a house, which was not very often, they all said, "Oh, *is* this it?" But it never was, till they reached the very top of the hill, just past the chalk-quarry and before you come to the gravel-pit. And then there was a white house with a green garden and an orchard beyond, and mother said, "Here we are!"

"How white the house is," said Robert.

"And look at the roses," said Anthea.

"And the plums," said Jane.

"It is rather decent," Cyril admitted.

The Baby said, "Wanty go walky;" and the fly stopped with a last rattle and jolt.

Everyone got its legs kicked or its feet trodden on in the scramble to get out of the carriage that very minute, but no one seemed to mind. Mother, curiously enough, was in no hurry to get out; and even when she had come down slowly and by the step, and with no jump at all, she seemed to wish to see the boxes carried in, and even to pay the driver, instead of joining in that first glorious rush round the garden and the orchard and the thorny, thistly, briery, brambly wilderness beyond the broken gate and the dry fountain at the side of the house. But the children were wiser, for once. It was not really a pretty house at all; it was quite ordinary, and mother thought it was rather inconvenient, and was quite annoyed at there being no shelves, to speak of, and hardly a cupboard in the place. Father used to say that the iron-work on the roof and coping was like an architect's nightmare. But the house was deep in the country, with no other house in sight, and the children had been in London for two years, without so much as once going to the seaside even for a day by an excursion train, and so the White House seemed to them a sort of Fairy Palace set down in an Earthly Paradise. For London is like prison for children, especially if their relations are not rich.

Of course there are the shops and theatres, and entertainments and things, but if your people are rather poor you don't get taken to the theatres; and you can't buy things out of the shops; and London has none of those nice things that children may play with without hurting the things or themselves – such as trees and sand and woods and waters. And nearly everything in London is the wrong sort of shape – all straight lines and flat streets, instead of being all sorts of odd shapes, like things are in the country. Trees are all different, as you know, and I am sure some tiresome person must have told you that there are no two blades of grass exactly alike. But in streets, where the blades of grass don't grow, everything is like everything else. This is why so many children who live in the towns are so extremely naughty. They do not know what is the matter with them, and no more do their fathers and mothers, aunts, uncles, cousins, tutors, governesses, and nurses; but I know. And so do you, now. Children in the country are naughty sometimes, too, but that is for quite different reasons.

The children had explored the gardens and the outhouses thoroughly before they were caught and cleaned for tea, and they saw quite well that they were certain to be happy at the White House. They thought so from the first moment, but when they found the back of the house covered with jasmine, all in white flower, and smelling like a bottle of the most expensive perfume that is ever given for a birthday present; and when they had seen the lawn, all green and smooth, and quite different from the brown grass in the gardens at Camden Town; and when they found the stable with a loft over it and some old hay still left, they were almost certain; and when Robert had found the broken swing and tumbled out of it and got a bump on his head the size of an egg, and Cyril had nipped his finger in the door of a hutch that seemed made to keep rabbits in, if you ever had any, they had no longer any doubts whatever.

The best part of it all was that there were no rules about not going to places and not doing things. In London almost everything is labelled "You mustn't touch," and though the label is invisible it's just as bad, because you know it's there, or if you don't you very soon get told.

Five Children and It by E. Nesbit

Questions

1 Locate and write a synonym for *'carriage'* in the first paragraph. [*1 mark*]

2 Which of these words is **not** a synonym for *'quarry'*?

mine   peak   pit [*1 mark*]

3 What did Mother find problematic about the house? [*1 mark*]

4 Explain what the phrase *'the scramble to get out of the carriage that very minute'* suggests about how the children were feeling. [*1 mark*]

5 How does the phrase *'The thorny, thistly, briery, brambly …'* improve our understanding of the wilderness beyond the gate? [*1 mark*]

6 What evidence is there that the White House was isolated? [*1 mark*]

7 How do we know that the family have been poor? Give **two** reasons. [*1 mark*]

8 Explain how the author's use of *'caught'* is effective for describing the children's behaviour. [*1 mark*]

9 *'London is like prison for children'*.
Find **three** examples of why London is not a good place for children to grow up. [*1 mark*]

10 The second-to-last paragraph has just two sentences, one of which is very long. Why do you think the author chose to write the sentence this way? [*3 marks*]

(1) hack   **1 mark** (Content Domain 2a)

(2) peak   **1 mark** (Content Domain 2a)

(3) There were no shelves and hardly any cupboards.   **1 mark** (Content Domain 2b)

(4) **Expected standard:** Pupils need to understand that scrambling to get out of the carriage infers that the children were very excited. The additional use of *'that very minute'* implies that they acted hastily and with urgency.   **1 mark** (Content Domain 2d)

(5) **Expected standard:** To answer this question, pupils need to be able to visualise the wilderness. Thorns, thistles, briars and brambles all grow on wild land and using these words as adjectives in this way creates a clear visual image of what the wilderness behind the house must have been like.   **1 mark** (Content Domain 2g)

(6) **Expected standard:** To answer this question, pupils need to understand the meaning of the word 'isolated'. They then need to use this to infer that lines such as *'The house was three miles from the station'* and *'the house was deep in the country, with no other house in sight'* imply that the house was isolated. Pupils should refer to the text in their answers.   **1 mark** (Content Domain 2d)

(7) **Expected standard:** To answer this question, pupils need to infer from several clues such as:
- they hadn't been to the seaside for two years;
- that London is like a prison if your relations are not rich;
- if your people are rather poor you don't get taken to the theatre or buy nice things.   **1 mark** (Content Domain 2d)

(8) **Expected standard:** Pupils should explain how the word *'caught'* suggests that the children's behaviour was wild and unrestrained. Accept answers that allude to the children being wild like animals.   **1 mark** (Content Domain 2g)

(9) **Expected standard:** Pupils need to read across the text to find examples of why London is not a good place for children to grow up. There are several references including:
- *'nearly everything in London is the wrong sort of shape'*;
- *'in streets, where the blades of grass don't grow, everything is like everything else'*;
- *'In London almost everything is labelled "You mustn't touch"'*.   **1 mark** (Content Domain 2f)

Expected standard: Pupils should explain how the sentence is a long list of things the children discovered and did on their arrival at the White House. By making the sentence so long the author has created a sense of excitement and emphasised the huge amount undertaken by the children in a short afternoon. **Up to 2 marks** (Content Domain 2g)

Extension: Some pupils may comment on the use of semi-colons to separate this list. They may also comment on how the list repeats *'and'*. Both of these features create pace, which reflects the children's excitement on arriving at the White House.

1 additional mark (Content Domain 2g)

Oddiputs

Even worried, solemn, six-year-old Bruno had to laugh when Sally did it. He knew it was naughty, worse than naughty – almost wicked. But he had to laugh because of Sally's face – her rosy, dimpled, sparkling-eyed, aren't-I-a-dear-little-girl face – as she said, 'Poor Oddiputs! Always so busy!'

And as she spoke, she tipped over Bruno's plate of breakfast cereal so that the mush of cornflakes and creamy milk and brown sugar made a wet, spreading, disgusting mess on the clean cloth on the nursery table. 'Oh dear, oh dearie me!' Sally said. Her eyes were very bright. 'Go on, Oddiputs! Clean it up!'

****

'Quick, Oddiputs!' Sally said. 'More to clear up! Look! Over here!' The robot turned; Sally cunningly used her spoon to spread the slush around, making sure that some of it messed the table as well as the tablecloth.

Bruno frowned. She was going too far. She was always going too far. But once again he had to smile when Oddiputs tried to catch up with Sally's spoon. The robot was too slow and clumsy. Now there was mush on the tablecloth, the table, the table legs. There was mush dribbling onto the carpet. The sticky patches spread.

****

In the small hours of the night, in the darkness of the passageway, Oddiputs' Watchdog unit sedately revolves, regularly, unhurriedly. Inside Oddiputs 'thoughts' surge and scamper. He thinks the thoughts are new each time he thinks them. They are not. They are the same old thoughts, always the same.

Yet they build. For each time he thinks them, the thoughts leave a tiny deposit on his hair-fine tapes. It is like a coral reef: the ages pass, the dead husks cement themselves together, the reef grows. With a robot, ages pass very, very quickly…

I am clean, Oddiputs thinks. Clean and correct…

And I am efficient. They are not efficient. When They were smaller (why do They need to change size and grow? *I* do not change *my* size!), They were always falling down. They were supposed to be like this I, but They fell down and became like this __. Then loud sounds would come out of their food-holes and their eyes would leak wetness. Sometimes their skin would split and leak red wetness. Then I had to 'clean the wound'. So the wound was dirty. They are dirty.

I have no wetnesses anywhere, ever.

I am Oddiputs.

They are only They…

He could think of so many things to prove his case:

My day is twenty-four hours. I do this and that and this. That is correct. That is efficient.

But They! They are alive for only fifteen or sixteen of the twenty-four hours. At night, They are as if dead. That is not efficient. So it cannot be correct.

And they are hot/cold. I am never hot/cold; always the same, always correct. I do not have coverings to put on and take off my body. They do. They have to wear clothes. *Cloe-th-sss.* That is hard to say. Sally teases me because I cannot say that word…

Oddiputs' mind tries to escape the thought of Sally and teasing. 'I am Oddiputs,' he recites, 'and They are only They.' This time, the good words do not work. So he decides to move his body – he is supposed to do this at intervals so that his various sealing rings will be freshly positioned and not become deformed.

As his body shifts, so does his 'mind'. A thought, a genuinely new thought, enters his head:

I am Oddiputs. They are only They. *Yet I serve them!*

The new thought astonishes him. It makes his head seem to bulge, his circuits and tapes seem to spin out of control. His 'mind' works on a binary, Go/No-Go system. The system seldom fails him. It fails him now. It will not answer the new thought:

I serve them. Why do I serve them? They are dirty, illogical, inefficient, insanitary, incorrect. They suffer hot/cold, They are always wanting things to put in their food-holes, They fall down. They shout and quarrel and suffer nightly death.

But I, Oddiputs – I am clean, effective, efficient, sanitary, unchanging – correct in every way. Perfectly correct.

So why do *I* serve *Them?*

Again and again Oddiputs consults his logic circuits, cuts in his memory stores, riffles through his programmes. No answer comes. Finally, desperately, he cross-indexes every faculty he possesses.

What humans would call a 'stroke' attacks him as the intricate mechanisms jam, fight, rebel – and fail.

Very briefly, his head actually warms. The Watchdog fails to revolve for a second or more. He clicks and whirrs and chitters. A tiny, ultrasonic scream issues from the grille protecting his vocalizer unit.

Then the cut-outs automatically operate, the circuits disentangle themselves, spools of gossamer cease to spin, transistors and silicon chips and microcircuits nod and bow to each other and say, 'After you, I insist' – and Oddiputs is himself again.

Himself, but not himself. Something extra has been added to his complicated make-up: a ray of dark light has entered him, a touch of original sin.

Oddiputs has somehow learned to envy – to despise – to hate.

Oddiputs by Nicholas Fisk

Questions

1 Which of the following are synonyms for *'gossamer'*?

delicate   fine   opaque   wispy   spidery   [1 mark]

2 When does Oddiputs do his thinking?   [1 mark]

3 Write **one** thing that Oddiputs thought proved he was efficient.   [1 mark]

4 Oddiputs appears *sedate* and *unhurried*, yet his thoughts *surge* and *scamper*. How does the choice of these words support what Oddiputs is and what takes place in the story?   [3 marks]

5 Who are the *'They'* that Oddiputs refers to? Why does the author use a capital letter when referring to them?   [2 marks]

6 Which of these quotations would you choose as the 'turning point' in the story? Explain your answer.   [2 marks]

		Tick one
A	I am efficient. They are not efficient.	
B	I am Oddiputs. They are only They. *Yet I serve them!*	
C	The system seldom fails him. It fails him now. It will not answer the new thought.	

7 Write down **one** piece of evidence from the text to show that Sally has been unkind to Oddiputs before.   [1 mark]

8 Look at the last three sentences of the story. How do you know that Oddiputs has become bad?   [2 marks]

9 What do you think Oddiputs will do next in the story? Refer to the text to support your answer.   [3 marks]

10 What does Oddiputs mean by these phrases?   [1 mark]

- *'loud sounds would come out of their food-holes'*;
- *'their eyes would leak wetness'*;
- *'their skin would split and leak red wetness'*.

Teaching assessment

(1) delicate, fine, wispy, spidery **1 mark for all four correct** (Content Domain 2a)

(2) Pupils should write that Oddiputs does his thinking in the small hours of the night. Accept in the early hours of the morning after midnight. **1 mark** (Content Domain 2b)

(3) Pupils should write one from:
- His day was 24 hours long (he was awake for 24 hours);
- He was never hot/cold (he was always the right temperature);
- He didn't need to wear clothes. **1 mark** (Content Domain 2b)

(4) **Expected standard:** Pupils should explain that Oddiputs is a robot. This means he carries out orders carefully and calmly. They should explain that robots cannot think for themselves but in the story Oddiputs learns to think and his thoughts race around his mind. It is not sufficient to say that he is calm on the outside and frantic on the inside without referring to the characteristics of robots and what takes place in the story. **Up to 3 marks** (Content Domain 2g)

(5) **Expected standard:** Pupils should be able to infer that *'They'* refers to the family and most specifically the children under Oddiputs' care. The author uses a capital to denote a proper noun. **1 mark** (Content Domain 2g)

Extension: Some pupils may also note that this is a stylistic device used by the author to make the words sound robot-like. **1 additional mark** (Content Domain 2g)

(6) **Expected standard:**

		Tick one
A	I am efficient. They are not efficient.	
B	I am Oddiputs. They are only They. *Yet I serve them!*	✓
C	The system seldom fails him. It fails him now. It will not answer the new thought.	

Pupils should be able to express that this is a genuinely new thought that enters Oddiputs' head (some pupils may quote from the preceding sentence where we are told this). It is after this thought that Oddiputs experiences his *'stroke'* and is left with his new dark ideas. **Up to 2 marks** (Content Domain 2f)

(7) **Expected standard:** Accept one of the following:
- *'She was going too far. She was always going too far.'*
- *'Sally teases me because I cannot say that word.'*
- *'Oddiputs' mind tries to escape the thought of Sally and teasing.'*

All of these quotations rely on pupils knowing synonyms for *'unkind'* and then being able to use them as evidence of Sally's previous unpleasant behaviour. **1 mark** (Content Domain 2d)

(8) **Expected standard:** Pupils should show their understanding of the phrases *'dark light'* and *'original sin'* which imply Oddiputs has become bad. They should also be able to share their understanding of the negative word choices *'envy'*, *'despise'* and *'hate'* as indications that Oddiputs has become bad.   **Up to 2 marks** (Content Domain 2d)

(9) **Expected standard:** Any reasonable answer based on information stated and implied in the text should be accepted. Award 1 mark for responses with single pieces of evidence from the text. E.g. *'Oddiputs has learned to hate. Therefore, I think he will seek his revenge on Sally.'*
                                                                        1 mark (Content Domain 2e)

Extension: Award up to 2 marks for fully developed responses. E.g. *Oddiputs has learned to envy, despise and hate. We know that he has had 'thoughts' about Sally's teasing so I think he will seek revenge on her for this. I think he will make her clean up her own mess and make her be more 'efficient'.*   **Up to 2 additional marks** (Content Domain 2e)

(10) **Expected standard:** To answer this question, pupils need to read the preceding sentences about the children falling when they were young. They should then be able to infer what is meant. Pupils' answers should include:
* The children would cry/the children's mouths opened and they cried/shouted;
* Tears came out of their eyes;
* They grazed or cut themselves and bled.   **1 mark** (Content Domain 2d)

Africa: Eye to Eye with the Unknown

Whistle down the wind

Blissfully unaware of a famous backdrop that includes a snow-topped Mt. Kenya and the rim of the Great Rift Valley, a lone bull giraffe stretches for the juiciest new leaves near the top of an acacia. It wraps its long and dextrous tongue around a sprig, seemingly immune to the tree's sharp thorns, some of which are 8 cm (3 inches) long. In fact, the giraffe has thick saliva and large papillae on its tongue that protect it and the inside of its mouth from the spines. It chews languidly and looks about haughtily, as only giraffes can, before returning to its chosen branch. Suddenly, it pulls back with unusual haste, shaking its head violently. It's made a mistake. It should have detected the tell-tale smell of the tiny creatures now making its life hell, but it failed to do so and is paying the price: ants with a very painful sting are attacking it.

The ants are in the protection racket. They live in bulbous swellings that join the shafts of several modified thorns, which the tree supplies along with free nectar at leaf bases; and all this in return for security services.

At the slightest hint of an intruder, like a giraffe that should have known better, the ants stream out from the galls and across branches ready to fight the monster to the death, but they don't attack every trespasser. They deal with the daily flood of leaf-eating insects, but they leave well alone insects that might pollinate the tree's flowers, and it's the tree that 'tells' them not to. The ants are allowed to protect the buds, but the freshly opened flowers (yet to be pollinated), produce a chemical that keeps the ants away, so any pollinators are not harmed. However, as soon as the flowers have been pollinated, the chemical restraint is removed and the ants can scramble over the flowers once more.

There are several species of acacia ants and the weaker ones prune buds to restrict side growth so that rival ant gangs on nearby trees cannot invade them and take over. The giraffe was confronted by the stronger and more aggressive type and on this day their less powerful neighbours have made a fatal mistake. They've overlooked a twig that's cracked and bent, creating a bridge between two trees. The invaders, ever eager to expand their territory, stream across, overwhelming the opposition in mandible-to-mandible and sting-to-sting fighting.

Ant attack

For sheer numbers there's a tiny creature in Africa's rainforests that's hard to beat. The first sign that it's about is a soft pitter-patter, like the sound of rain, but it's not water that's falling, it's ants – driver ants, the dreaded *siafu* – probably the most feared ants on the planet.

These ants are an advance party that's been foraging in the trees, searching for anything that's living; anything that can be sliced and diced and carried back to their bivouac a kilometre away. They crawled up the trunk from the forest floor, but having swept the tree clean of its resident insects, they find the quickest way down – and that's to drop – so it's raining ants.

They cannot see. They have no eyes. They follow scent trails on the ground and up through the trees. Their entire life is governed by smell. The scouts lay the first trails and the others follow, an army that moves through the forest at about 20 m (65 feet) per hour. When a caterpillar or other juicy creature is found, the aggressive workers – each no longer than 0.5 cm (0.2 inches) – emit an alarm odour that encourages many others to come running and to launch an attack. Soon the target is completely smothered by a squirming mass of black bodies, each worker equipped with razor-sharp mandibles for cutting through flesh like a knife through butter.

Large soldier ants, each 1.5 cm (0.6 inches) long and armed with enormous jaws, line the supply columns to protect the busy workers as they run frantically between the front line and the bivouac. The nest itself is made from the living bodies of ants. Inside are living corridors and chambers, all made of ants.

The innermost sanctuary contains the gigantic queen and her consort. At 5.5 cm (2.2 inches) long, she's the largest ant in the world. She lays 1–2 million eggs every month, the hatching grubs attended by nursery workers who feed them with meat brought back by the rest of the foraging workers.

There are so many of them – over 20 million in a single colony – and they are such efficient killers that they can strip a patch of forest of its small animals – earthworms, insects, spiders, scorpions and sometimes even nestlings and small mammals – in a few days, and then be forced to move on to find new feeding grounds elsewhere.

Moving the bivouac is a major military manoeuvre. First the scouts find a suitable campsite, and then the rest of the army follows. They travel along an avenue lined by soldiers. They even form a living roof across open ground, so the rest of the moving colony is safe. The smaller workers carry eggs and larvae delicately in their jaws, passing rapidly along the makeshift corridor in a continuous stream and depositing them in the nursery at the new nest site. Last to leave the old site is the queen. When she arrives at the new location, the avenue breaks down and the daily massacre resumes, the workers stripping bare another part of the forest.

Africa: Eye to Eye with the Unknown by Michael Bright

Questions

1 Write down **two** things the text tells you about the protective features of giraffes' mouths.   [1 mark]

2 Copy the paragraph headings into your book and match to the correct paragraph number.   [1 mark]

Heading	Paragraph number
How trees talk to ants	5
Raining ants	3
Moving the colony	1
A giraffe is left with a bad taste in its mouth	11

3 Find a word in the first paragraph that means 'lacking force or quickness of movement'.   [1 mark]

4 The author tells us that *'The ants are in the protection racket'*. Explain how the ants protect the acacia tree.   [1 mark]

5 What does the phrase *'innermost sanctuary'* suggest about the home of the driver ant queen?   [2 marks]

6 What is the driver ants' bivouac made from? Copy the sentence that tells you this.   [1 mark]

7 These words and phrases come from the passage about driver ants:
- *launch an attack;*
- *front line;*
- *military manoeuvre;*
- *massacre.*

What impression do they give you of the characteristics of a driver ant colony?   [2 marks]

8 Compare how chemical communication is used by acacia ants and driver ants.   [2 marks]

9 Why do you think the author suggests *siafu* are probably the most feared ants on the planet? Give at least **three** reasons from the text.   [3 marks]

10 Find evidence in the text to show why a bivouac is the most suitable home for driver ants.   [3 marks]

1 thick saliva, large papillae 　　　　　　　　　　**1 mark** (Content Domain 2b)

2 This question asks pupils to consider the whole text and match the following paragraphs to the headings:

Heading	Paragraph number
How trees talk to ants	3
Raining ants	5
Moving the colony	11
A giraffe is left with a bad taste in its mouth	1

1 mark for all four correct (Content Domain 2c)

3 languidly 　　　　　　　　　　　　　　　　**1 mark** (Content Domain 2a)

4 This question asks pupils to apply their understanding of words and phrases in context and to retrieve information showing how the ants protect the acacia tree. Pupils should note that the ants attack predators.

E.g. *A protection racket is a group that provides violent protection for somebody else. The ants kill or injure other creatures that threaten the acacia tree so are like a protection racket.* Pupils may refer to the giraffe or leaf-eating insects in their response.

1 mark (Content Domain 2b)

5 **Expected standard:** Pupils should refer to '*innermost*' indicating that it is positioned at the heart of the bivouac and so furthest away from threat/harm. 　**1 mark** (Content Domain 2d)

Extension: Some pupils may refer to '*sanctuary*' as a word meaning a place of safety. Some pupils may even refer to the notion of 'taking sanctuary' as a way of being protected from an attack. 　　　　　　　　　　　　　　**1 additional mark** (Content Domain 2d)

6 Pupils need to make a connection between 'bivouac' and 'nest' in order to answer this question. E.g. *The bivouac is made from the bodies of the ants. The sentence that tells us this is: 'The nest itself is made from the living bodies of ants.'* 　　**1 mark** (Content Domain 2b)

7 **Expected standard:** This question requires pupils to consider the words chosen by the author and the impact of these on the overall meaning. Pupils should refer to the military association of the words and phrases. They should explain that the use of these words reinforces the organisation and behaviour of the ants. Accept the words 'army' and 'military' in pupils' responses. 　　　　　　　　　　　　　　　　**Up to 2 marks** (Content Domain 2g)

(8) **Expected standard:** This question offers pupils the opportunity to compare information from the two sections of the text. Pupils should compare how the acacia ants read signals left by the acacia tree, whereas driver ants produce their own chemical messages in order to be able to communicate with one another. **Up to 2 marks** (Content Domain 2h)

(9) **Expected standard:** Pupils should give three reasons why people may fear *siafu*. Accept any reasonable evidence from the text such as:

- They drop from trees. The thought of ants dropping from trees and landing on people could be frightening;
- The size of the colony (20 million ants) is huge and could fill people with fear;
- Their ability to strip a patch of forest in just a few days is a terrifying thought;
- The sight of the bivouac moving from one location to another could be frightening to many people. **Up to 3 marks** (Content Domain 2d)

(10) **Expected standard:** This question requires pupils to read across the section about driver ants. They need to retrieve key information and use this to infer why driver ants need to constantly move their nest. They should refer to the need to move easily to find more food as a result of the colony's huge numbers and massive appetite. **1 mark** (Content Domain 2f)

Extension: Some pupils may clarify their response by pointing to evidence such as the ants' ability to eat huge numbers of creatures in a short amount of time and the sheer numbers in their colony which would make a stationary home unsuitable. E.g. *A bivouac is far more suitable to the siafu than an ordinary nest. The text tells us that there are 'Over 20 million in a single colony' and that they can 'strip a patch of forest of its small animals' in just a few days. If they were not able to move so easily then the colony would die. This is why a bivouac suits them best.* **Up to 2 additional marks** (Content Domain 2f)

Fenn Halflin and the Fearzero

Halflin huffed and dug deep inside the bag, pulling the other papers out and passing them over. Viktor scrutinised them carefully; nodding, holding them up to the light, one by one, checking each watermark. At last he stuffed both permits into the top of his jacket, thrust the ID back at Halflin and nodded curtly to Fenn. Then he gave Halflin a quick, strange glance; half smile, half scowl, and disappeared back up the gangplank.

Now alone, Fenn turned to Halflin, a quizzical look in his eyes.

It had come. The moment of truth. He was sending the boy away and he must never return. Halflin never wanted him back; it was too dangerous on East Marsh. It was more than the right time; it was the perfect moment to tell him he wasn't his grandfather and that they meant nothing to each other. Now was the time to say he was just an unlucky Sunkyard owner who saved a lucky child, kept him safe and hidden as best as he could, made him strong and healthy, taught him as much as he could to survive, but did not mollycoddle him nor weaken him with love. The time had come to cut him – like he'd cut his webbed toes thirteen years before. It would be for his own good.

Cut him loose. Cut him free. Cut him clean away forever.

Say it! Halflin thought. *Say it!*

But he couldn't. His throat had turned to lead and his tongue seemed to shrivel in his mouth, shrinking from the words it had to speak. On board the crew were preparing to cast off and whistled at them to hurry. Fenn looked at Halflin expectantly, but the moment had gone.

"Do we board?" he asked, searching Halflin's face for answers. A sudden scatter of icy rain speckled the water and his teeth began chattering. He was frozen and exhausted. Halflin tucked the ID card in Fenn's shirt pocket and patted it to make sure it was safe.

"Grandad?"

"Warm enough? It'll be clap cold offshore," Halflin said gruffly. Something cracked in his voice. "Best ter keep warm."

Halflin shrugged off his heavy reefer jacket, hanging it on the twigs of Fenn's shoulders. It was damp from the marsh and weighed a tonne; Fenn's puny frame buckled beneath the load, but it was warm. As he dipped under its weight, he felt the truth dawn on him.

"You're not coming are you?"

Halflin concentrated on jamming the buttons through their holes.

"Pigs'll nee feedin'."

His voice had taken on a different tone; lighter than usual. He squeezed the last button into its place and jerked his head towards the boat. "Viktor'll take yer to our kin. Won't take long; four weeks if the weather holds. Bit longer if yer hit storms."

"I'm not going without you!" Fenn said stubbornly. Halflin glared at him.

"You'll do as I tell yer!" he said, trying to keep the shaking out of his voice. "Don't yer see? I've never left the Sunkyard, not fer one night, not in thirteen year. If I come wiv yer, Chilstone will smell a rat! Then they'll be lookin' fer an ol' man an' a kid. We'll stick ou' like a shark's fin. Yer safer alone."

Halflin managed to winch the sides of his mouth up to make an almost convincing smile.

"An' I'm safest stayin' put," he said, knowing that was what the boy needed to hear. "Anyhow, won' be forever," he finished with a nod.

It would be forever. Halflin would make sure of that.

For a moment Fenn looked like he was about to cry and for a second Halflin softened, but he shook it off as quickly as it had come. He took Fenn's shoulders firmly in his hands.

"Now don't go blubbin'; it'll jus' make yer feel worse... Viktor's all right. Do as 'e tells yer," Halflin said, staring hard into Fenn's eyes. Fenn nodded, though his lips were quivering. The boat's engine suddenly snapped into life again and the *Panimengro* shuddered and rattled as the propeller turned.

"Spies are everywhere, throw 'em off the scent. Tell everyone yer fifteen! Best ter go older; folks will jus' think yer a runt. Don't forget wha' I told yer, but bury it! Bury it deep. Chilstone will hunt yer down and kill yer if 'e finds out, so trust no one an' nothin'...'cept yer instinct. Got it?" With each instruction he roughly shook Fenn's shoulders.

Fenn nodded obediently and reached out to hug him, but Halflin held firm against affection; it helped no one. Instead he put his arm out, like a battering ram, and pressed the flat of his huge hand on Fenn's chest as if trying to drive caution into his very heart. Before Fenn knew what was happening, Halflin had spun him on the spot towards the ship and pushed him along the gangplank.

Fenn Halflin and the Fearzero by Francesca Armour-Chelu

1. Which of the following words or phrases are synonyms for *'mollycoddle'*?

   pamper   neglect   wrap in cotton wool   indulge   protect   [*1 mark*]

2. Complete the table about characters in the story.   [*1 mark*]

Name	Description
Halflin	
	Halflin's 'grandson'
Viktor	
	Fenn's enemy

3. Read the paragraph beginning: *'It had come…'*. Write down **three** things that we discover about Halflin.   [*1 mark*]

4. What evidence is there to tell us that Fenn was thin? Find **three** examples.   [*1 mark*]

5. *'Halflin managed to winch the sides of his mouth up to make an almost convincing smile.'*
   What does this phrase imply about Halflin's feelings about Fenn's safety?   [*3 marks*]

6. What does *'Something cracked in his voice'* tell us about how Halflin was feeling?   [*1 mark*]

7. Do you think that Halflin will feel upset when Fenn has gone? Explain your answer by referring to the text.   [*1 mark*]

8. How does the phrase *'his tongue seemed to shrivel in his mouth, shrinking from the words it had to speak,'* describe how Halflin was feeling?   [*3 marks*]

9. Across the text the author uses words such as *'Halflin said gruffly'*, *'Halflin glared'*, *he roughly shook'*. How do these words reflect how Halflin cared for Fenn?   [*1 mark*]

Teaching assessment

1 pamper, wrap in cotton wool, indulge **1 mark for all three correct** (Content Domain 2a)

2

Name	Description
Halflin	Sunkyard owner (and Fenn's 'grandad')
Fenn	Halflin's 'grandson'
Viktor	Captain of the *Panimengro*
Chilstone	Fenn's enemy

1 mark for all four correct (Content Domain 2b)

3 Pupils should provide three pieces of evidence about Halflin, such as:

- he wasn't Fenn's grandfather;
- he was the Sunkyard owner;
- he'd rescued Fenn;
- he'd kept him safe;
- he'd *'made him strong and healthy'*;
- he'd taught him how to survive;
- he'd not mollycoddled him;
- he'd cut Fenn's webbed toes. **1 mark for three examples** (Content Domain 2b)

4 **Expected standard:** Pupils should locate the following the following evidence from the text:

- *'the twigs of Fenn's shoulders'*;
- *'Fenn's puny frame'*;
- *'As he dipped under its weight'*.

To answer this question, pupils need to activate both their understanding of vocabulary and how Fenn's reactions are indicative of his physical size and strength.

1 mark (Content Domain 2d)

5 **Expected standard:** Pupils should explain that *'winch[ing] up the sides of his mouth'* implies that he had to force himself to smile with some effort and that forcing himself to smile implies that it was not genuine. Some pupils may be able to explain that the use of *'almost convincing'* implies that the smile was unconvincing. This then shows that Halflin was unconvinced about Fenn's safety. **Up to 3 marks** (Content Domain 2d)

6 **Expected standard:** Pupils should be able to infer that Halflin's voice cracking is a sign that he is upset. **1 mark** (Content Domain 2d)

7 **Expected standard:** Accept any reasonable response supported by at least one piece of evidence from the text. E.g. *I think Halflin will be upset when Fenn has gone because although he tries to convince himself that 'he doesn't love the boy, 'his throat turned to lead and his tongue seemed to shrivel in his mouth' when he tried to tell Fenn that he wasn't his grandad.*

1 mark (Content Domain 2e)

(8) **Expected standard:** To answer this question, pupils need to understand the word *'shrivel'* and how this would make his tongue smaller or make it 'shrink'. They should try to explain that shrivelling would make Halflin's tongue shrink in size. They should then explain that this physical description represents how he was avoiding telling Fenn the truth.

Up to 2 marks (Content Domain 2g)

Extension: Some pupils may also be able to explain how the phrase *'to shrink away from'* implies being frightened of something. By doing this they should be able to explain how Halflin feared telling Fenn the truth. **1 additional mark** (Content Domain 2g)

(9) **Expected standard:** Pupils need to explain how being *'gruff'* and *'rough'*, and *'glaring'*, are reflective of the way that Halflin cared for Fenn – in a firm but loving way. They should draw on information from the early part of the text where Halflin says how he had cared for the boy but he hadn't mollycoddled him or weakened him with love. **1 mark** (Content Domain 2g)

Cowboy Song

I come from Salem County

    Where the silver melons grow,

Where the wheat is sweet as an angel's feet

    And the zithering zephyrs blow.

I walk the blue bone-orchard

    In the apple-blossom snow,

Where the teasy bees take their honeyed ease

    And the marmalade moon hangs low.

My Maw sleeps prone on the prairie

    In a boulder eiderdown,

Where the pickled stars in their little jam-jars

    Hang in a hoop to town.

I haven't seen Paw since a Sunday

    In eighteen seventy-three

When he packed his snap in a bitty mess-trap

    And said he'd be home by tea.

Fled is my fancy sister

    All weeping like the willow.

And dead is the brother I loved like no other

    Who once did share my pillow.

I fly the florid water

    Where run the seven geese round,

O the townsfolk talk to see me walk

    Six inches off the ground.

Across the map of midnight

    I trawl the turning sky,

In my green glass the salt fleets pass,

    The moon her fire-float by.

The girls go gay in the valley

    When the boys come down from the farm,

Don't run, my joy, from a poor cowboy,

    I won't do you no harm.

The bread of my twentieth birthday

    I buttered with the sun,

Though I sharpen my eyes with lovers' lies

    I'll never see twenty-one.

Light is my shirt with lilies,

    And lined with lead my hood,

On my face as I pass is a plate of brass,

    And my suit is made of wood.

Cowboy Song by Charles Causley

1 Match each word to its definition and write them in your book. [*1 mark*]

zephyrs	a large rock, typically worn smooth by erosion
boulder	lying flat, especially face downwards
prone	soft gentle breezes
zither	a stringed musical instrument

2 Where does the cowboy come from? [*1 mark*]

3 Decide whether each statement about the poem is true or false. [*1 mark*]

	True	False
The townsfolk talk to the cowboy when he visits town.		
The cowboy's mother is buried beneath boulders.		
One Sunday, the cowboy's father left the family home and did not return.		
The cowboy and his brother once shared a bed.		

4 Why do you think the girls run from the cowboy? [*1 mark*]

5 What evidence is there in the poem that the cowboy could be lonely? Give **three** reasons. [*2 marks*]

6 What is the suit that the cowboy refers to in the final line of the poem? [*1 mark*]

7 How is the mood of the opening stanza enhanced through the description: '*the zithering zephyrs blow*'? [*3 marks*]

8 What do you think the poet means by a '*bone-orchard*'? [*1 mark*]

9 '*I walk … I fly … I trawl … I pass*' – how do the use of these words work to suggest that the cowboy is restless? [*1 mark*]

10 Who do you think has left the lilies on the cowboy's grave? Use at least **one** piece of evidence from the text to support your opinion. [*2 marks*]

Teaching assessment

(1)

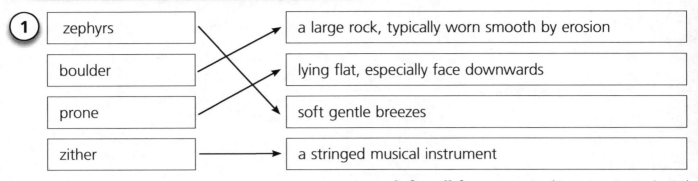

zephyrs	a large rock, typically worn smooth by erosion
boulder	lying flat, especially face downwards
prone	soft gentle breezes
zither	a stringed musical instrument

1 mark for all four correct (Content Domain 2a)

(2) Salem County

1 mark (Content Domain 2b)

(3)

	True	False
The townsfolk talk to the cowboy when he visits town.		✓
The cowboy's mother is buried beneath boulders.	✓	
One Sunday, the cowboy's father left the family home and did not return.	✓	
The cowboy and his brother once shared a bed.	✓	

1 mark for all four correct (Content Domain 2c)

(4) **Expected standard:** Pupils should explain that the girls run away from him because he is a ghost, and they're frightened of him. In order to answer this question, pupils need to read the whole text and infer from a variety of clues that the cowboy is a ghost.

1 mark (Content Domain 2d)

(5) **Expected standard:** Pupils need to infer that the cowboy could be lonely because he's on his own. Reasons could include:
- His mother is dead and buried on the prairie;
- He hasn't seen his father since 1873;
- His sister has run away;
- His brother is dead;
- The girls run away from his ghost;
- He was on his own on his 20th birthday.   **Up to 2 marks** (Content Domain 2d)

(6) **Expected standard:** To answer this question, pupils need to infer that the wooden suit is the cowboy's coffin. Answering this question requires them to draw on the three preceding lines, which describe his grave.   **1 mark** (Content Domain 2d)

(7) Expected standard: To answer this question, pupils need to explain that *'zithering zephyrs'* suggests a light musical breeze and this adds to the sense of calm and serenity in the opening stanza.   **1 mark** (Content Domain 2g)

Extension: Some pupils may be able to further explain that the poet has used alliteration, which draws the reader's attention to the description. They may also be able to refer to the use of short vowel sounds in both of these words, which enhances the idea of a light breeze.
                                                                    Up to 2 additional marks (Content Domain 2g)

(8) Expected standard: Pupils should infer that *'bone-orchard'* means a graveyard.
                                                                    1 mark (Content Domain 2d)

(9) Expected standard: Pupils need to recognise that each word suggests movement and that this indicates that the cowboy is constantly roaming his environment.
                                                                    1 mark (Content Domain 2g)

(10) Expected standard: This is an open question that asks the pupils to make a prediction based upon what they have read. Accept any reasonable answer that is accompanied by evidence from the text. E.g. *I think it was his sister. We know that his mother and brother are dead and he says that he hasn't seen his father since 1873.*   **1 mark** (Content Domain 2e)

Extension: Some pupils may also say he refers to his sister as having fled rather than being dead. He also uses the present tense to refer to her, which suggests she may still be alive. He also says that she is weeping – perhaps this is for his loss. Accept alternative suggestions if accompanied with evidence from the text.   **1 additional mark** (Content Domain 2e)

One morning, at a little before seven o'clock, I was awakened by the maid tapping at the door, to announce that two men had come from Paddington, and were waiting in the consulting room. I dressed hurriedly, for I knew by experience that railway cases were seldom trivial, and hastened downstairs. As I descended, my old ally, the guard, came out of the room, and closed the door tightly behind him.

'I've got him here,' he whispered, jerking his thumb over his shoulder; 'he's all right.'

'What is it, then?' I asked, for his manner suggested that it was some strange creature which he had caged up in my room.

'It's a new patient,' he whispered, 'I thought I'd bring him round myself; then he couldn't slip away. There he is, all safe and sound. I must go now, Doctor, I have my dooties, just the same as you.' And off he went, this trusty tout, without even giving me time to thank him.

I entered my consulting room, and found a gentleman seated by the table. He was quietly dressed in a suit of heather tweed, with a soft cloth cap, which he had laid down upon my books. Round one of his hands he had a handkerchief wrapped, which was mottled all over with blood-stains. He was young, not more than five-and-twenty, I should say, with a strong masculine face; but he was exceedingly pale, and gave me the impression of a man who was suffering from some strong agitation, which it took all his strength of mind to control.

'I am sorry to knock you up so early, Doctor,' said he. 'But I have had a very serious accident during the night. I came in by train this morning, and on inquiring at Paddington as to where I might find a doctor, a worthy fellow very kindly escorted me here. I gave the maid a card, but I see that she has left it upon the side table.'

I took it up and glanced at it. 'Mr Victor Hatherley, hydraulic engineer, 16a Victoria Street (3rd floor).' That was the name, style, and abode of my morning visitor. 'I regret that I have kept you waiting,' said I, sitting down in my library chair. 'You are fresh from a night journey, I understand, which is in itself a monotonous occupation.'

'Oh, my night could not be called monotonous,' said he, and laughed. He laughed very heartily, with a high ringing note, leaning back in his chair, and shaking his sides. All my medical instincts rose up against that laugh.

'Stop it!' I cried. 'Pull yourself together!' And I poured some water from a carafe.

It was useless, however. He was off in one of those hysterical outbursts which come upon a strong nature when some great crisis is over and gone. Presently he came to himself once more, very weary and blushing hotly.

'I have been making a fool of myself,' he gasped.

'Not at all. Drink this!' I dashed some brandy into the water, and the colour began to come back to his bloodless cheeks.

'That's better!' said he. 'And now, Doctor, perhaps you would kindly attend to my thumb, or rather to the place where my thumb used to be.'

He unwound the handkerchief and held out his hand. It gave even my hardened nerves a shudder to look at it.

'Good heavens!' I cried, 'this is a terrible injury. It must have bled considerably.'

'Yes, it did. I fainted when it was done; and I think that I must have been senseless for a long time. When I came to, I found that it was still bleeding, so I tied one end of my handkerchief very tightly round the wrist, and braced it up with a twig.'

'Excellent! You should have been a surgeon.'

'It is a question of hydraulics, you see, and came within my own province.'

'This has been done,' said I, examining the wound, 'by a very heavy and sharp instrument.'

'A thing like a cleaver,' said he.

'An accident, I presume?'

'By no means.'

'What, a murderous attack!'

'Very murderous indeed.'

'You horrify me.'

I sponged the wound, cleaned it, dressed it; and, finally, covered it over with cotton wadding and carbolized bandages. He lay back without wincing, though he bit his lip from time to time.

'How is that?' I asked, when I had finished.

'Capital! Between your brandy and your bandage, I feel a new man. I was very weak, but I have had a good deal to go through.'

'Perhaps you had better not speak of the matter. It is evidently trying to your nerves.'

'Oh, no; not now. I shall have to tell my tale to the police; but, between ourselves, if it were not for the convincing evidence of this wound of mine, I should be surprised if they believed my statement, for it is a very extraordinary one, and I have not much in the way of proof with which to back it up. And, even if they believe me, the clues which I can give them are so vague that it is a question whether justice will be done.'

The Great Adventures of Sherlock Holmes: The Engineer's Thumb by Sir Arthur Conan Doyle

1 Which of the following is **not** a synonym for *'monotonous'*?

boring   repetitive   invigorating   dreary   uneventful   *[1 mark]*

2 About how old does the doctor think the visitor is?   *[1 mark]*

3 Decide whether each statement about the extract is true or false.   *[1 mark]*

	True	False
The engineer was escorted to the doctor's by a train guard.		
Victor's injury took place overnight.		
Victor was reluctant to tell the police about his injury.		

4 Read the first paragraph. How did the doctor know that the patient would be in serious need of medical support?   *[1 mark]*

5 What has happened to Victor's thumb? Find and copy a phrase that tells you this.
                                                                                    [2 marks]

6 What did Victor do that prompted the doctor to say that he should have been a surgeon?   *[1 mark]*

7 What impression does the author's use of *'quietly dressed'* give you about Victor?   *[1 mark]*

8 The doctor says to Victor: *'Perhaps you had better not speak of the matter. It is evidently trying to your nerves.'* What behaviour of Victor's is the doctor referring to?
                                                                                    [3 marks]

9 When writing about the moment of Victor's injury the author uses the passive voice: *'Yes, it did. I fainted when it was done.'* Why do you think he chose to do this?
                                                                                    [1 mark]

10 *'He lay back without wincing, though he bit his lip from time to time.'* What impression does this phrase give you about Victor's reaction to pain?   *[1 mark]*

(1) invigorating

1 mark (Content Domain 2a)

(2) 25 (accept younger than 25). Pupils should look for the phrase *'not more than five-and-twenty'*.

1 mark (Content Domain 2b)

(3)

	True	False
The engineer was escorted to the doctor's by a train guard.	✓	
Victor's injury took place overnight.	✓	
Victor was reluctant to tell the police about his injury.		✓

1 mark for all three correct (Content Domain 2c)

(4) **Expected standard:** To answer this question, pupils need to recognise how *'for I knew by experience that railway cases were seldom trivial'* indicates that the doctor was drawing on his experience of previous patients. To do this they need to know that 'serious' is an antonym of 'trivial'.

1 mark (Content Domain 2d)

(5) **Expected standard:** Victor's thumb has been cut off. The phrase telling us this is:
'And now, Doctor, perhaps you would kindly attend to my thumb, or rather to the place where my thumb used to be.'
This question asks pupils to infer that *'the place where my thumb used to be'* means that the thumb is no longer there.

1 mark (Content Domain 2d)

Extension: Some pupils may refer forward in the text to the point where Victor and the doctor discuss the implement used to inflict the injury as part of their inference.

1 additional mark (Content Domain 2d)

(6) Pupils should explain that Victor bound and splinted his own wound.

1 mark (Content Domain 2b)

(7) **Expected standard:** This question requires pupils to understand that *'quietly dressed'* is an idiomatic phrase meaning that someone is dressed conservatively. Accept responses that allude to Victor being understated, lacking flamboyancy, introverted rather than extroverted, and not wishing to stand out or draw attention to himself.   **1 mark** (Content Domain 2g)

(8) **Expected standard:** Pupils should refer to the point in the text where Victor started to laugh. They should draw on the doctor's view that, *'He was off in one of those hysterical outbursts which come upon a strong nature when some great crisis is over and gone.'*
This question requires pupils to make links between different points in the text. In doing this they need to connect the phrase *'trying to your nerves'* with the hysterical laughter and shaking that had overcome Victor earlier in the narrative. **Up to 3 marks** (Content Domain 2f)

(9) **Expected standard:** Pupils should be able to explain that the use of the passive voice removes the subject (actor) of the sentence. By doing this, the author has created a sense of mystery or suspense in that we don't know how the injury was sustained, or who did it.
                                                                     1 mark (Content Domain 2g)

(10) **Expected standard:** Pupils should be able to explain that Victor was brave or stoical in the face of pain because he avoided reacting to the intervention of the doctor. To answer this question, pupils need to understand the meaning of *'wince'*. They also need to be able to infer that by biting his lip Victor did feel pain but was trying not to show it.
                                                                     1 mark (Content Domain 2g)

The Tempest

Dramatis Personae:

Alonso, King of Naples

Sebastian, his brother

Antonio, his brother, the usurping Duke of Milan

Ferdinand, son to the King of Naples

Gonzalo, an honest old councillor

Master of a ship

Boatswain

Mariners

THE SCENE: *A ship at sea; afterwards an uninhabited island*

ACT I SCENE I   *On a ship at sea: a tempestuous noise of thunder and lightning heard*

[*Enter a Master and a Boatswain*]

Master	Boatswain!
Boatswain	Here, master: what cheer?
Master	Good, speak to the mariners: fall to't, yarely, or we run ourselves aground: bestir, bestir.

[*Exit Master*]

[*Enter Mariners*]

Boatswain	Heigh, my hearts! cheerly, cheerly, my hearts! yare, yare! Take in the topsail. Tend to the master's whistle. Blow, till thou burst thy wind, if room enough!

[*Enter ALONSO, SEBASTIAN, ANTONIO, FERDINAND, GONZALO, and others*]

ALONSO	Good boatswain, have care. Where's the master? Play the men.
Boatswain	I pray now, keep below.
ANTONIO	Where is the master, boatswain?
Boatswain	Do you not hear him? You mar our labour: keep your cabins: you do assist the storm.
GONZALO	Nay, good, be patient.
Boatswain	When the sea is. Hence! What cares these roarers for the name of king? To cabin: silence! trouble us not.
GONZALO	Good, yet remember whom thou hast aboard.
Boatswain	None that I more love than myself. You are a counsellor; if you can command these elements to silence, and work the peace of the present, we will not hand a rope more; use your authority: if you cannot, give thanks you have lived so long, and make yourself ready in your cabin for the mischance of the hour, if it so hap. Cheerly, good hearts! Out of our way, I say.

[*Exit*]

GONZALO	I have great comfort from this fellow: methinks he hath no drowning mark upon him; his complexion is perfect gallows. Stand fast, good Fate, to his hanging: make the rope of his destiny our cable, for our own doth little advantage. If he be not born to be hanged, our case is miserable.

[*Exeunt*]

Re-enter Boatswain]

Boatswain	Down with the topmast! yare! lower, lower! Bring her to try with main-course.

[*A cry within*]

A plague upon this howling! they are louder than the weather or our office.

[*Re-enter SEBASTIAN, ANTONIO, and GONZALO*]

Yet again! what do you here? Shall we give o'er and drown?
Have you a mind to sink?

SEBASTIAN	A pox o' your throat, you bawling, blasphemous, incharitable dog!
Boatswain	Work you then.
ANTONIO	Hang, cur! hang, you whoreson, insolent noisemaker!
	We are less afraid to be drowned than thou art.
GONZALO	I'll warrant him for drowning; though the ship were no stronger than a nutshell and as leaky as an unstanched wench.
Boatswain	Lay her a-hold, a-hold! set her two courses off to sea again; lay her off.

[*Enter Mariners, wet*]

Mariners	All lost! to prayers, to prayers! all lost!
Boatswain	What, must our mouths be cold?
GONZALO	The king and prince at prayers! let's assist them,
	For our case is as theirs.
SEBASTIAN	I'm out of patience.
ANTONIO	We are merely cheated of our lives by drunkards:
	This wide-chapp'd rascal–would thou mightst lie drowning
	The washing of ten tides!
GONZALO	He'll be hang'd yet,
	Though every drop of water swear against it
	And gape at widest to glut him.

[*A confused noise within:* 'Mercy on us!'– 'We split, we split!'–'Farewell, my wife and children!'– 'Farewell, brother!'–'We split, we split, we split!']

ANTONIO	Let's all sink with the king.
SEBASTIAN	Let's take leave of him.

[*Exeunt ANTONIO and SEBASTIAN*]

GONZALO	Now would I give a thousand furlongs of sea for an acre of barren ground, long heath, brown furze, any thing. The wills above be done! but I would fain die a dry death.

[*Exeunt*]

The Tempest by William Shakespeare

Questions

(1) Find and copy a synonym for 'sailors'. [1 mark]

(2) Where does this scene take place? [1 mark]

(3) Decide whether each statement about the extract is true or false. [1 mark]

	True	False
The crew are instructed to take action to prevent the ship from running aground.		
The King tells the Boatswain he will be hanged when they return to land.		
The passengers get in the way of the crew, which makes it hard for them to do their jobs.		
There is a huge sound and voices shout that the ship is splitting.		

(4) What does the Boatswain mean when he tells the passengers 'you do assist the storm'? [1 mark]

(5) Find and copy the words that show us that Gonzalo would rather die on land than at sea. [1 mark]

(6) Explain how Shakespeare's use of 'whistle', 'blow' and 'roarers' in the actors' lines enhances what is taking place on the ship. [1 mark]

(7) What do the following phrases tell you about the Boatswain's feelings towards the passengers?
- 'You mar our labour: keep your cabins...';
- 'To cabin: silence! trouble us not.';
- 'Out of our way, I say.' [1 mark]

(8) The first line of the play is a stage instruction: 'On a ship at sea: a tempestuous noise of thunder and lightning heard'. What do you think would happen in the theatre at this point? [1 mark]

(9) Explain how this stage instruction contributes to what is taking place in the scene: [A confused noise within: 'Mercy on us!'– 'We split, we split!'–'Farewell, my wife and children!'– 'Farewell, brother!'–'We split, we split, we split!'] [3 marks]

(10) What do you infer about how the passengers are feeling from these lines?

A plague upon this howling! they are louder than the weather or our office. [2 marks]

Teaching assessment

Supporting pupils to read and understand play scripts

When answering questions about play scripts, encourage pupils to read the extract all the way through first. Encourage them to read the lines in conjunction with the stage directions in order to understand more about where the action is taking place and how the characters are feeling. Pupils should also note any lighting or sound effects described in the script and consider how these contribute to the meaning of the extract. Pupils are now ready to start answering questions about the text.

About this scene

The action takes place on a small ship during a huge storm: a tempest. The scene starts with the sound of thunder and lightning followed by the Captain asking the Boatswain to rouse the Mariners to prevent the ship from being run aground. Chaos ensues, which is compounded by the arrival of the Noble Passengers on the deck. As the passengers go below decks, and then back above, tensions flare between the Boatswain and the Nobles. Eventually there is the sound of cracking, which we can assume is the ship breaking up in the storm.

A number of websites provide detailed summaries of scenes from Shakespeare's plays and/or modern line-by-line translations. Refer to these if more support is needed.

(1) mariners **1 mark** (Content Domain 2a)

(2) The scene takes place on a ship at sea. **1 mark** (Content Domain 2b)

(3)

	True	False
The crew are instructed to take action to prevent the ship from running aground.	✓	
The King tells the Boatswain he will be hanged when they return to land.		✓
The passengers get in the way of the crew, which makes it hard for them to do their jobs.	✓	
There is a huge sound and voices shout that the ship is splitting.	✓	

1 mark for all four correct (Content Domain 2c)

(4) **Expected standard:** To answer this question, pupils need to infer that the passengers are hindering the crew in their battle against the storm. Accept answers which allude to the passengers getting in the way or preventing the crew from doing their work.

1 mark (Content Domain 2d)

(5) Pupils should quote from Gonzalo's speech at the end of the scene:
Now would I give a thousand furlongs of sea for an acre of barren ground, long heath, brown furze, any thing. The wills above be done! but I would fain die a dry death.

Accept answers that take key words from this speech without copying it in full.

1 mark (Content Domain 2b)

(6) **Expected standard:** Pupils should explain how *'whistle'*, *'blow'* and *'roarers'* are words associated with the wind. As the ship is battling in a tempestuous storm in this scene, the choice of these words enhances the strength and presence of the wind.

1 mark (Content Domain 2g)

(7) **Expected standard:** To answer this question, pupils need to infer that the Boatswain feels the passengers are a nuisance. Accept answers such as 'he feels the passengers are getting in the way'.

1 mark (Content Domain 2d)

(8) **Expected standard:** Pupils should be able to predict that there would be the sound of thunder and the effect of lightning in the theatre.

1 mark (Content Domain 2e)

(9) **Expected standard:** Pupils should be able to explain that at this point in the play the characters are frightened and unsure about what is taking place. The instruction to shout *'we split, we split'* adds to the sense of chaos on the ship.

1 mark (Content Domain 2f)

Extension: Some pupils may be able to explain that the audience is unsure as to who is speaking, which further adds to the uncertainty. They may also point to the use of 'confused noise' as a direction to create a sense of chaos, which enhances the action that is taking place.

Up to 2 additional marks (Content Domain 2f)

(10) **Expected standard:** To answer this question, pupils need to activate their understanding of the word 'howling'. From this they should be able to infer that the passengers are frightened. Some pupils may also note that the words are preceded by the stage instruction *[a cry within]*, which further indicates that the passengers are fearful. **Up to 2 marks** (Content Domain 2d)

Acknowledgements

The author and publisher are grateful to the copyright holders for permission to use quoted material.

Every effort has been made to trace copyright holders and obtain their permission for the use of copyright material. The author and publisher will gladly receive information enabling them to rectify any error or omission in subsequent editions.

Romulus and Remus from *The Orchard Book of Roman Myths* by Geraldine McCaughrean, © Geraldine McCaughrean 1999, reproduced by permission of Orchard Books, an imprint of Hachette Children's Group, Carmelite House, 50 Victoria Embankment, London, EC4Y 0DZ

When Hitler Stole Pink Rabbit by Judith Kerr. Reprinted by permission of HarperCollins Publishers Ltd. © 1971 Judith Kerr

The Purple Lady from *Blackberry Blue and Other Fairy Tales* by Jamila Gavin. Reproduced by permission of Tamarind

I Am Malala: The Girl Who Stood Up for Education and Was Shot by the Taliban by Malala Yousafzai with Christina Lamb. Copyright © 2013 by Salarzai Limited. Used by permission of Little, Brown and Company

The Visitor © Estate of Ian Serraillier

The Mystery of the Clockwork Sparrow by Katherine Woodfine. Text copyright © 2015 Katherine Woodfine. Published by Egmont UK Ltd and used with permission

Arthur: High King of Britain by Michael Morpurgo. Reproduced by permission of Egmont

The Cloudspotter's Guide 2006 © Gavin Pretor Pinney. Reproduced by permission of Hodder and Stoughton Limited

Extract from short story Oddiputs © Nicholas Fisk from *Sweets from a Stranger and Other Science Fiction Stories* (Viking Children's Books, 1982). Reprinted by permission of the Estate

Africa: Eye to Eye with the Unknown by Michael Bright, reproduced by permission of Quercus.

Fenn Halflin and the Fearzero © 2016 Francesca Armour-Chelu. Reproduced by permission of Walker Books Ltd, London SE11 5HJ. www.walker.co.uk

Cowboy Song by Charles Causley from *Collected Poems for Children*. Published by Macmillan Children's Books and used with permission

Published by Keen Kite Books
An imprint of HarperCollins*Publishers* Ltd
1 London Bridge Street
London
SE1 9GF

Text and design © 2017 Keen Kite Books, an imprint of HarperCollins*Publishers* Ltd

10 9 8 7 6 5 4 3 2 1

ISBN 978-0 00 821883 6

The author asserts their moral right to be identified as the author of this work.

British Library Cataloguing in Publication Data
A catalogue record for this publication is available from the British Library.

Author and Series Editor: Rachel Clarke
Commissioning Editors: Michelle I'Anson and Shelley Teasdale
Project Management: Fiona Watson
Editor: Rebecca Adlard
Cover Design: Anthony Godber
Internal design and illustrations: QBS Learning
Production: Paul Harding